Boeing
747 SP
By Brian Baum

Great Airliners Series

Volume Three

About The Author

Brian Baum was born in Seattle in 1959 and grew up with a keen interest in aviation, particularly commercial airlines and airliners. His appreciation of the special abilities of the 747SP began aboard Pan American's Flight 50 in 1977 – the first passenger flight around the world over both the North and South Poles. He serves as Public Programs Manager at the Museum of Flight in Seattle, where he is responsible for adult educational programming. This occupation has allowed him the pleasure of bringing many of the greatest names in aviation history to lecture at the Museum. He enjoys travel, photography, and flying in aircraft of all types. His logbook is filled with hundreds of entries which include flights in the 247D, Ju 52, B-17, Constellation and Concorde. He now lives with his wife Úna, and their cats, in West Seattle.

© 1997 by Brian Baum
All rights reserved.
ISBN 0-9626730-7-2
First Edition September 1997
Printed and bound in Hong Kong

No part of this publication may be reproduced, stored in a retrieval system, or transmitted by any means without first seeking written permission of the publisher.

The publisher acknowledges that certain terms, logos, names, and model designations are property of the trademark holder. They are used here for correct identification purposes only.

All information contained in this volume is accurate at the time of publication.

Series Editor: Jon Proctor

Book and cover design by Randy Wilhelm, Keokee Company, Sandpoint, Idaho
Copy Editors: Fred Chan, Hollis Palmer, Billie Jean Plaster

Front cover photo courtesy of The Boeing Company
Title page photo courtesy of Julian Green
Back cover photo courtesy of The Boeing Company Archives
Inside back cover photo by Jeffrey S. DeVore

The Great Airliners series:
  Volume One: *Convair 880/990,* by Jon Proctor
  Volume Two: *Douglas DC-8,* by Terry Waddington
  Volume Three: *Boeing 747SP,* by Brian Baum
  Volume Four: *McDonnell Douglas DC-9,* by Terry Waddington

Table of Contents

Acknowledgments 4

Introduction 5

Chapter I .... *Concept and Development* 6

Chapter II .... *Assembly and Rollout* 10

Chapter III .... *Flight Test* 13

Chapter IV .... *747/747SP Comparison* 19

Chapter V .... *Marketing the 747SP* 26

Chapter VI .... *The Record Setter* 42

Chapter VII .... *Initial Operators* 47

Chapter VIII .... *Inside the 747SP* 60

Chapter IX .... *747SP Pictorial History* 71

Chapter X .... *Safety* 114

Chapter XI .... *The Future* 115

Appendices

Appendix I .... *Individual Aircraft Disposition* 118

Appendix II .... *Aircraft Names* 126

Appendix III .... *Registration Index* 127

Appendix IV .... *Bibliography* 128

Acknowledgments

The author would like to acknowledge all those involved in helping put this book together. Few things in life are better than that indescribable feeling of achievement after one has searched endlessly for an elusive piece of the puzzle – whether it is a much coveted photograph or a tiny tidbit of historic information – and then it suddenly becomes available through the generosity of someone allowing access to their personal collection. In the production of this book I have become deeply indebted to many people around the world for providing such valuable assistance.

Special thanks to Jon Proctor of World Transport Press for having the faith that I could indeed produce this book, and then providing the unlimited support necessary to help me complete it. Tom Lubbesmeyer and Mike Lombardi of The Boeing Company Historical Archives for their willingness to let me dig through 25 years of archival records and hundreds of photographs in my search for the facts. Dennis Parks, Senior Curator of the Museum of Flight, for the trust to let me make use of the Museum's many treasures. Fred Chan and Hollis Palmer, who spent way too much of their valuable time proof reading. Aviation artist and dear friend, Mike Machat, who assisted this effort with illustrations and provided much needed guidance. Gary Jones of Westgate Travel, for demonstrating how truly successful one can be with a great deal of hard work, dedicaton and a good sense of humor.

My sincere appreciation to Andrew Gleadow of Airclaims Ltd. for allowing access to their indispensable Client Aviation System Enquiry database for publication of the aircraft event histories. David J. Tamer of The Boeing Company also deserves thanks and acknowledgment for his enthusiastic assistance with obtaining the Airclaims information.

I would also like to acknowledge the following Boeing employees for providing their support: Brian Ames, William Francoeur, Tom Hanser, Robert W. Hegge, Alwyn T. Lloyd, Jake Schultz and Jay P. Spenser. Research assistance was received from Alison G. Bailey, Christine R. Francoeur, Elizabeth Furlow, Norm Kirby, David Morse, Frédéric Pralus, Christine Runte, David Turner, Ben Valley and Nicholas A. Veronico.

Jan Mogren and Tommy Mogren were especially generous with sharing their outstanding SP photo archives. The mountains of data they have compiled on the history of the SP provided much appreciated verification for my research. Maurice Bertrand and Jay Selman went way above and beyond the call to assist with locating critical photographs.

I am grateful to AP/Wide World Photos, John Adkins, ATP/Airliners America, Jean-Luc Altherr, Jonny Andersson, Mike Axe, Paul Bannwarth, J.-F. Boussouge, Ed Davies, Jeffrey S. DeVore, Bruce Drum, Roberto Farina, Max Fankhauser, Brian J. Gore, Julian Green, Eddy Gual, Brian Gustafson, Bill Hough, John Kitchen, Eric LeGendre, Michael McLaughlin, Jean M. Magendie, Matthew Martin, K. Nakano, Fred Nott, Akinobu Okuda, Joe Pries, Barry Roop, SPA Photography, Nicky Scherrer, H. J. Schroeder, Bob Shane, Robbie Shaw, A.J. Smith, Jerry Stanick, Duncan Stewart, John Stewart, Edwin Terbeek, Jim Thompson, Eric M. Trum, Christian Volpati, Terry Waddington, Robert A. Woodling and Jorge Zmich for making their photographs available.

Lastly, I would like to thank three very special people in my life. My wife, Úna, for her almost unlimited patience with me and my annoying research and writing habits. Most especially, I am forever indebted to the two people who encouraged me most in my interests: my mother, Joanna, for allowing her young aviation-minded son the freedom to roam the streets of downtown Seattle in search of the numerous airline sales offices and their vast wealth of collectibles; and my father Howard, to whom this book is dedicated, for sharing his lifelong love of aviation with me.

Thank you, I could not have done it without you.

Brian Baum
Seattle, Washington

My father, Howard Baum, (fourth from left) and his fellow wind tunnel employees, show off a 777 flutter model to legendary Boeing test pilot A.M. "Tex" Johnston, center, in his customary Stetson. (The Boeing Company)

INTRODUCTION

Upon first glance, the Boeing 747SP seems to be an unremarkable airplane. Selling only 45 copies in 16 years between the go-ahead announcement and final delivery, the SP certainly did not set any sales records. Boeing's high hopes for the SP – predicting as many as a half dozen variants coming down the production line for 20 years – never materialized. Commonly called "stubby" because of its wide, short fuselage and huge wings, it is certainly far from being the sleekest airliner ever built.

Yet the "Junior Jumbo" is as beautiful, as reliable, and as safe as any of the legendary commercial transports. It performed as advertised, easily flying the longest, thinnest routes years before there was any competition to match it. The SP was a pathfinder, setting numerous speed and distance records – many of which still stand today – including three spectacular flights around the world. It flew higher, faster and farther than any of its subsonic contemporaries. Perhaps most importantly for Boeing, the SP was used by many of the operators as an entry into the 747 series, paving the way for a large number of future sales and giving these and other customers reason to avoid purchasing wide-body equipment from the competition.

Once offered as a replacement for the presidential VC-137s, the SP is now coveted by many governments around the world as the ultimate VIP aircraft for their leaders, a role which should continue long after the SPs have left regular airline service. These statesmen know that the 747 is still the most imposing and impressive passenger-carrying aircraft available. The National Aeronautics and Space Administration (NASA) is currently in the process of modifying an SP to carry a 98-inch telescope to altitudes between 41,000 and 45,000 feet, a job which the little 747 is uniquely suited to fly.

My research on the history of the 747SP brought to mind many similarities with another long-range Boeing airliner, the Model 377 Stratocruiser. When compared to its more graceful rivals, the DC-7 and Constellation, the Stratocruiser fuselage seemed rather rotund. Despite outward appearances, the main cabin was comfortable, roomy and luxurious – passengers wishing to stretch their legs could even take a spiral staircase to relax in a lower deck lounge. Only 55 production model Stratocruisers were delivered, with Pan American placing the initial and largest order. Even though it did not sell as well as Boeing had hoped, the Stratocruisers faithfully served their original and subsequent operators for many years and established a well-earned place on most enthusiasts' short list of great airliners.

Even though the first 747SPs are now being broken up for spare parts and scrap metal, it seems certain that the remaining aircraft will have a long and productive future in service. And perhaps, like the Stratocruiser, the 747SP will receive appropriate recognition for its role in the development of commercial aviation.

(Boeing Junior Jumbo sticker courtesy of Ben Valley)

Chapter I
CONCEPT AND DEVELOPMENT

Artist's concept of the 747SP. Because the basic premise for the aircraft was well-defined from the start, the initial design of the SP and the finished product remained outwardly similar. (The Boeing Company Archives)

The Requirement

The early 1970s found The Boeing Company without an aircraft suitable for longer, medium-density flights to fill the niche between the aging, narrow-body 707, and the high-capacity 747 jumbo jet. Boeing was losing customers to McDonnell Douglas which was offering its DC-10 wide-body tri-jet and finding success with carriers already flying the 747. At the same time, Lockheed was developing the L-1011 TriStar for this lucrative market. While acknowledging that airlines were looking for a fuel efficient, long-range aircraft with good performance, Boeing also took note of surveys which indicated the passenger's preference for a four-engine, wide-body for transoceanic flights. In the late 1960s and early 1970s, Boeing had studied – and discarded – several twin-jet and tri-jet designs based on the 747 to fill this need. The aircraft design that the Seattle aerospace giant finally came up with in 1973 looked as if it had the potential to deliver just about everything the major carriers were looking for.

Boeing engineers believed that creating an entirely new aircraft design was unnecessary, since they already had the foundation for what was needed with the basic 747. Taking the existing airframe and reducing its length by 48 feet provided a size and capacity equivalent to the McDonnell Douglas and Lockheed tri-jets. The design featured a mixed-class passenger capacity of 288 and high-density, all-economy seating for up to 360 – or about 100 fewer than the standard 747. Basing this new airplane on an existing design would provide exceptional parts commonality and cost savings to airlines already operating or planning to operate the full-size 747. The concept allowed numerous opportunities to reduce weight – at a gross weight of 650,000 pounds, the smaller aircraft would be almost 125,000 pounds lighter than the (then) heaviest long-range 747. When coupled with an estimated 20 percent lower fuel consumption and the 747's powerful engines, the new jet would provide unmatched speed, performance and range. Having the ability to fly almost 7,000 miles while carrying a substantial payload would create new nonstop markets around the world. This fresh design also allowed for very smooth high-altitude flights. The anticipated cruising levels would be 4,000 to 6,000 feet higher than any other subsonic airliner, allowing it to overfly slower traffic on congested routes. Dollar-per-mile costs were estimated to be equivalent to the long-range tri-jets, with seat-mile costs expected to be lower than any competitively sized airplane.

Decision to Proceed

After several months of studies, wind tunnel tests and concept ideas, Boeing management made the decision to proceed "incrementally" with the new aircraft program in June 1973. The numbers must have been right because the official go-ahead announcement for the development of Boeing's "747 Special Performance," or 747SP, was released just two months later, on August 23, 1973. During the earliest stages of development the new reduced length fuselage design was known by the less glamorous (and less marketable) working name 747SB, or "Short Body."

Boeing took a substantial risk by embarking on this program without prior commitment from the airlines for a minimum number of aircraft, although at the time of the official announcement it was in promising sales negotiations with several airlines – including the two largest operators of 747s – Pan American and Japan Air Lines. On September 10, 1973, these negotiations led to the first firm order. Pan American agreed to buy 10 of the new Special Performance 747s, with options for 15 more. Purchase price for the 10 aircraft was $280 million, including spares. E.H. Boullioun, President of Boeing Commercial Airplane Company, stated "The program is on schedule; all we needed to get rolling towards production was that order from Pan American."

Boeing projected the long-term sales strength for the SP to be very good, with many imaginative applications to maintain production for as long as 20 years. These applications potentially included as many as a half-dozen versions of the SP to be placed in competition with the wide-body tri-jets and as replacements for older DC-8s and 707s. While the stated objective of the SP was to meet airline requirements for markets with traffic densities between those of the basic 747 and the 707, Boeing's emphasis was placed on providing range capabilities superior to all other airliners, while at the same time offering unmatched takeoff, cruise altitude and

Boeing analyst Howard Martin (left) and sales representative Hank Wilder discuss the interior configuration of the SP during initial development. The large-scale cutaway model featured the new longitudinal galley and first-class seating in Zones A, B, and the upper deck. (The Boeing Company)

speed capability. Other concepts under study included a variant for use on short-to-medium-range routes to replace 707s and DC-8s and to compete with the latest designs from Long Beach and Palmdale. High-profile applications for which the SP would be suited included replacing the presidential VC-137s and serving as a luxurious VIP aircraft for leaders around the world – particularly in the oil-rich Middle East. A version carrying a mix of 194 passengers and 1,512 cubic feet of main deck cargo (using the existing Number Four entry door) would also be considered, as well as studies which added a large main-deck cargo door for oversized pallets.

Final assembly of the SP would take place in the massive 200-million-square-foot 747 division plant at Paine Field in Everett, Washington, about 30 miles north of Seattle. Because of the differences in production flow time between the new SP and the full-size models, a second 747 assembly line was to be reactivated exclusively for SP final assembly. Originally used during the early years of the 747 program, the second (east) assembly bay had been closed when standard 747 production rates dropped.

By April 1974, only eight months after the official go-ahead, the Special Performance project was in full swing: The SP design had been fully defined, fabrication of parts had begun, and specifications for the Pan American and Iran Air versions (still the only two customers to have placed orders at this date) were completed. Japan Air Lines announced it had decided to add the SP to its fleet of 747s, although no firm orders had yet been received. Detailed engineering drawings for the structure were partially finished, and a comprehensive series of wind tunnel tests continued. Progress on the engineering mockup proceeded on schedule, with all equipment due to be installed by late June 1974. An innovative interior mockup had been completed in December 1973. As part of the design process, pilots could now "fly" the SP in a special simulator to anticipate what its handling traits would be like when compared to those of the standard 747. In all, over 600 designers and engineers, along with several hundred other employees and over a dozen major subcontractors, were assigned to the SP program. Development cost for the 747SP program was substantial, although no official totals have been released. One estimate places the figure at $100 million. Boeing management was pleased with the progress made to this point and expressed a great deal of confidence in their new "Junior Jumbo," as the project remained on schedule for rollout in May 1975.

Wind Tunnel Testing

The 747SP design was thoroughly tested in low- and high-speed wind tunnels over a 19-month period from April 1973 to November 1974. SP drag factors were determined by re-testing the basic 747 model, testing the SP model, and then applying the differences to original 747 flight test results. Evaluation of the SP's flutter characteristics proved better than anticipated. These tests showed the ability of the structure to function safely under all required conditions.

High-speed wind tunnel tests included initial SP characteristics, aft body development and loads, vertical tail loads, rudder development, wing-body fairings, aerodynamic refinement, and complete configuration drag confirmation. Low-speed trials focused on flutter, flap development and loads, low-speed flying characteristics, the extended horizontal tail, and stability and control simulation. Wind tunnel tests also indicated that the SP's low-speed drag would be less than originally quoted for the aircraft.

Engineering Mockup

As part of the program to develop the first 747, a full-size static-test airframe was "flown" for over 60,000 hours, over a two-year period, to locate potential weaknesses in the structure. Subjected to loads far in excess of those which 747s would encounter in normal airline service, the airframe provided a number of modifications which were incorporated into future aircraft. Fatigue testing of the

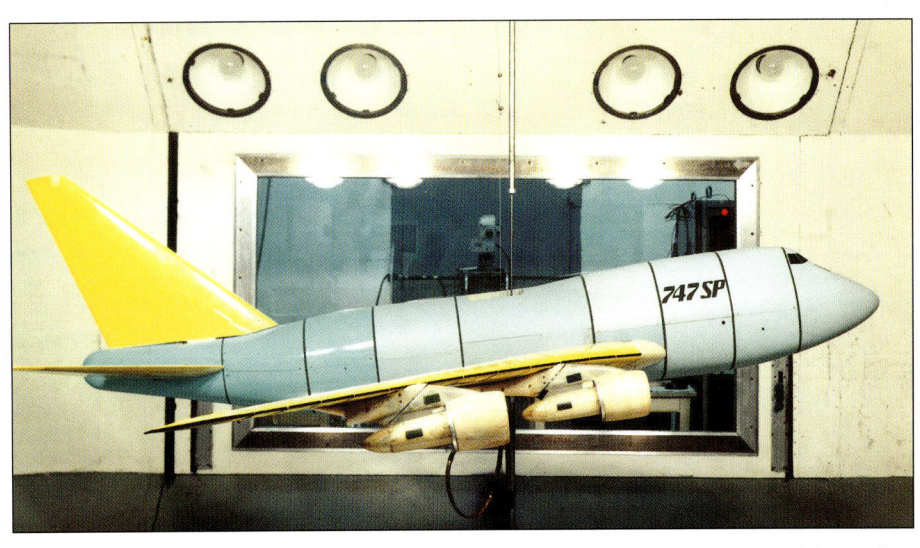

Boeing 747SP flutter model in a low-speed wind tunnel test. The segmented scale model actually "flies" to test the structural dynamics of the aircraft. (Museum of Flight Archives)

airframe took place in a cage-like structure mounted on a three-foot-thick concrete apron adjacent to the assembly building. In 1970, at the completion of the static test program, the retired fuselage was placed into storage.

When the 747SP program was approved three years later, the static test airframe was brought back to serve as the major part of the engineering mockup for development of interiors and systems for the SP. The airframe provided a real airplane structure as the basis for the mockup, which made it possible for the exact fitting of equipment and parts, including rigging of the flight controls. Body sections were removed from in front of and from behind the wing, and a new aft fuselage section was manufactured.

Work on the mockup was completed the following summer, and within one year after it was resurrected from storage, all wiring, tubing, control cables, and insulation were installed for testing. The right wing was attached to the fuselage for testing, including the layout of the lighter variable pivot trailing edge flaps. Joseph Sutter, Vice President and General Manager of the 747 Division, called the mockup "the best we've ever had at Boeing." Because of its somewhat advanced age, the SP mockup featured the early 747 three-window arrangement on either side of the upper deck, rather than the 10 windows incorporated on the production model. Following the initial development work, the mockup became a manufacturing support facility for the program.

Interior Mockup

The original full-scale 747 interior mockup, located at the Boeing Renton facility, was also adjusted to fit the needs of the SP program. Built in 1967 to develop the seating and in-flight service layouts for the standard 747, the mockup had since been used to test new interior features, to take sales promotional photographs, and to allow customers to visualize interior arrangements and decor for their aircraft prior to production.

To make the best use of the SP's new fuselage length, the design was developed as a cooperative effort between Boeing interior engineers, airline personnel and longtime Boeing design consultants, Walter Dorwin Teague Associates. A major innovation for the cabin crew was the longitudinal (or side facing) forward galley, which allowed the crew to serve first-class passengers from the forward end and economy-class from the aft. Developed with input from airline cabin service staff, the galley offered extra room, convenience, and privacy for the crews. A cart lift to the aft galley service center on the upper deck, a second main deck galley located just ahead of the aft pressure bulkhead, and overhead stowage bins in both main deck galleys were also new features on the SP. The placement of the two main galleys was planned to avoid interference with passenger loading and unloading, which meant quicker servicing and reduced time on the ground.

The mockup was divided into four main deck service zones, which also corresponded to the four major body sections of the aircraft at final assembly. Zone A was the first-class section and offered 28 passengers a spacious layout free of galleys, lavatories and flight crew traffic. Zone B included an additional 16 first-class seats, the forward galley and two lavatories. Even with the large side facing galley, Zone B passenger seating was equivalent to the number possible with a conventional galley and could be changed from first-class to economy seating as required. The wall separating passengers

The production airframe originally used for the 747 static test program found new life as the SP engineering mockup. The photograph shows the 747 fuselage cut down to size, prior to the installation of the two center access doors and the addition of the modified aft fuselage section. (The Boeing Company)

The first-class section of the full-scale interior mockup featured vivid, trendy colors. The forward galley is behind the reflective cabin panel on the far right. (The Boeing Company)

from the galley on the mockup was finished with "a decorative laminate, giving the impression of translucence." Zone C featured 136 economy seats, and Zone D could seat 86 economy passengers in a 10-abreast layout. Three economy-class lavatories were located between Zones B and C, and four between Zones C and D.

In the style of the '70s, colors in the interior mockup featured extremely bright, "modern" tones throughout the cabin. First-class sections had gold and brown carpet, cabin paneling in gold with silver, and the large, comfortable seats varied in color from light to deep shades of orange. Economy-class sections were carpeted in brown, with seats and cabin panels in blue-green, blue, red-orange, red and gold. Wall panels throughout the mockup were silver and beige.

Flight Comparison Simulator

From the beginning, Boeing included the pilot in the design process so that the airplane systems could be modified to meet the requirements of the flight crew. To identify and compensate for any handling differences in the SP, Boeing pilots logged hundreds of hours in a new state-of-the-art engineering simulator, comparing the characteristics between the standard and Special Performance 747s. These "flight comparisons" were made by using computer programs which duplicated the responses of the two aircraft during takeoffs, climbouts, cruising at various speeds, approaches and landings. Data from the simulator was used in the design process, allowing Boeing to tailor and adjust the fully powered control system before the first flight was made. The aim of the flight comparison program was to make the handling characteristics of the SP so much like those of the original that 747 pilots only required ground school and simulator time to be checked out and qualified on the smaller aircraft.

Responses from the two aircraft were programmed in an Electronic Associates Inc. 8400 computer, making it possible for pilots to "fly" a certain test condition in the SP and seconds later to "fly" the same condition in the standard 747. Effects simulated included autothrottle, speedbrakes, flaps, landing gear, wheel brakes, nose-wheel steering and thrust reversers. Views of takeoffs and landings were simulated by use of a rear-projected image of a runway.

Approximately 300 hours of comparison flights took place in the months prior to the first flight. In addition to Boeing personnel, pilots from airlines ordering the SP were also included in the comparison tests to assist with their transition to the new aircraft.

The interior mockup's innovative longitudinal galley provided a large, well-lit space for flight attendants to work. Rows of modular carts simplified meal service. (The Boeing Company)

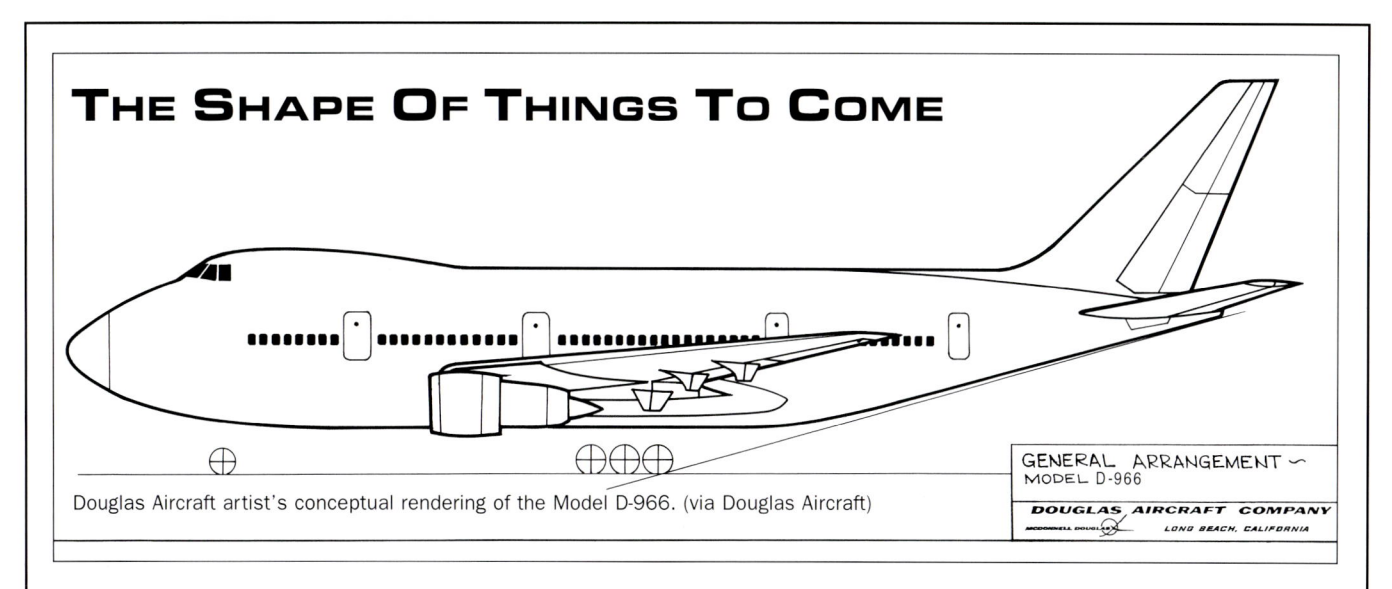

THE SHAPE OF THINGS TO COME

Douglas Aircraft artist's conceptual rendering of the Model D-966. (via Douglas Aircraft)

GENERAL ARRANGEMENT — MODEL D-966
DOUGLAS AIRCRAFT COMPANY
LONG BEACH, CALIFORNIA

In 1966, Douglas Aircraft prepared several designs for a medium-range, wide-body aircraft to fulfill a request made by American Airlines. Submitted for consideration were several twin-jet and tri-jet concepts, including the double-decked Douglas D-966. Because an all-cargo variant of the D-966 was planned, the flight deck was placed above the main cabin to allow for the loading of containers through a nose cargo door.

The D-966 and the Boeing 747SP, although conceived to fly entirely different types of routes, are remarkably similar in size and shape. The D-966 was to carry as many as 332 passengers, and its 184-foot, 6-inch fuselage would have been just 3 inches shorter than the SP. Eventually Douglas selected a tri-jet design which evolved into the DC-10/MD-11 series, and the D-966 concept was discarded.

Chapter II
ASSEMBLY AND ROLLOUT

In just a 10-hour period, the five major body sections and the wings of the first 747SP (ln 265/msn 21022) were joined. If you look closely, you can see where each of these sections met (see the sectional breakdown graphic on the following page). Sections 41 and 42 (being lifted by crane) were previously mated just ahead of the first upper deck window. Section 44 had already been attached to the wings, and sections 46 and 48 were joined just aft of the Number Four entry door. (Museum of Flight Archives)

Assembly Sequence

Major assembly of the first 747SP – line number (ln) 265, manufacturer's serial number (msn) 21022 – began on November 5, 1974, with construction of the first two wing sections at the Everett Division plant. Fabrication of parts began seven months prior with components manufactured by Boeing and supplied by vendors from around the world. Like the larger 747, sub-contractors built and shipped some of the largest sections of the aircraft. For example, Boeing-Wichita built the cockpit section, Boeing-Winnipeg assembled the fiberglass honeycomb wing-to-body fairings, and the entire tail section (except for the dorsal fin and rudder) was built by Vought Systems in Texas. Northrop constructed components for the main fuselage sections in California. Pratt and Whitney built the JT9D engines in Connecticut. In all, 17 major (and numerous minor) subcontractors supplied components to build the SP. Many of these sections were shipped to Everett in special railroad cars via routes that avoided bridges and tunnels too small for the large cargo.

Three-and-one-half months later, on February 21, 1975, the left and right wing were joined to the wing center section. This assembly then moved to the "clean, seal and paint" position for completion. Meanwhile, the five major body sections were built up at the sub-assembly locations. The manufacturing sequence for the first SP took place as follows (refer to the sectional breakdown on the next page): The wings were assembled and were joined to the wing center section. Body Section 44 (center) was assembled and mated with the completed wings to create the center body. The ailerons, engine struts, outboard flaps, spoilers, wing leading edges and wing tips were all added at this time. Body Sections 41 (nose) and 42 (forward) were assembled separately and then joined to form the forward body.

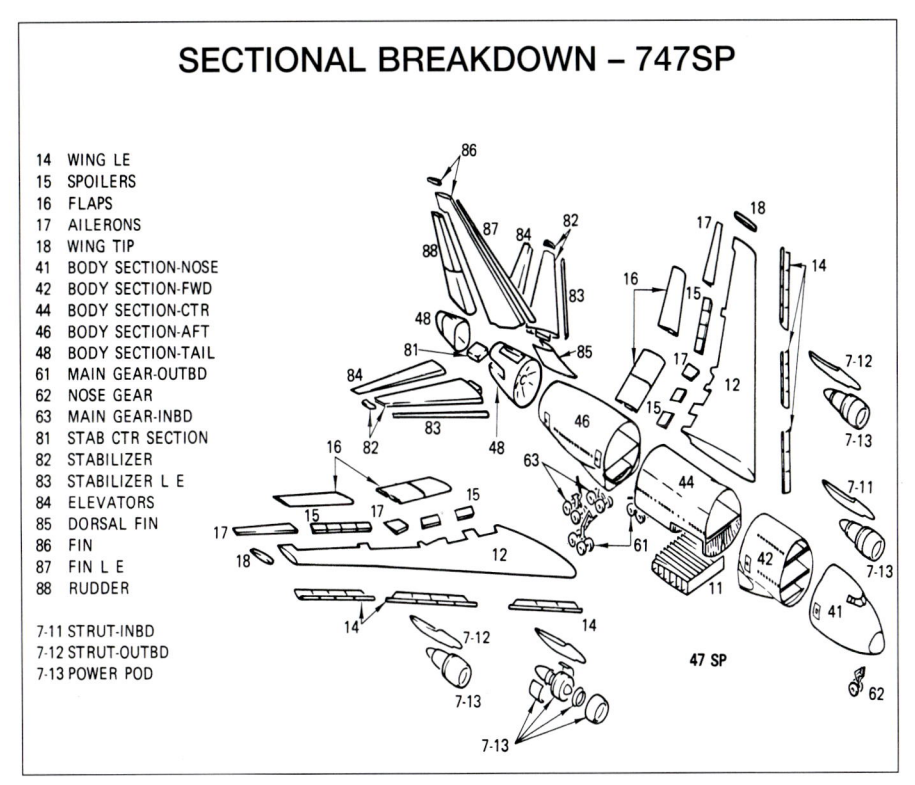

SECTIONAL BREAKDOWN – 747SP

14	WING LE
15	SPOILERS
16	FLAPS
17	AILERONS
18	WING TIP
41	BODY SECTION-NOSE
42	BODY SECTION-FWD
44	BODY SECTION-CTR
46	BODY SECTION-AFT
48	BODY SECTION-TAIL
61	MAIN GEAR-OUTBD
62	NOSE GEAR
63	MAIN GEAR-INBD
81	STAB CTR SECTION
82	STABILIZER
83	STABILIZER L E
84	ELEVATORS
85	DORSAL FIN
86	FIN
87	FIN L E
88	RUDDER
7-11	STRUT-INBD
7-12	STRUT-OUTBD
7-13	POWER POD

11	Wing center section
12	Wing structure
14	Wing leading edge
15	Spoilers
16	Flaps
17	Ailerons
18	Wing tip
41	Body section (nose)
42	Body section (forward)
44	Body section (center)
46	Body section (aft)
48	Body section (tail)
61	Main gear (outboard)
62	Nose gear
63	Main gear (inboard)
81	Stabilizer center section
82	Stabilizer
83	Stabilizer leading edge
84	Elevators
85	Dorsal fin
86	Fin
87	Fin leading edge
88	Rudder
7-11	Strut (inboard)
7-12	Strut (outboard)
7-13	Power pod

Sectional breakdown of the 747SP's major components. In addition to Boeing, numerous subcontractors manufactured sub-assemblies, and shipped these sections prior to final construction of the aircraft at Everett. (Museum of Flight Archives)

Sections 46 (aft) and 48 (tail) were also produced in the same way as 41 and 42, making the aft body. This left just three major components remaining to be assembled. All of this came together in a period of only 10 hours. Beginning at midnight, March 19, 1975, the three fuselage and wing sections were lifted into place, creating the giant form of a new aircraft. Huge overhead cranes lifted the forward and aft bodies onto cradles to be fitted together with the center body, which was already in place on the factory floor. This delicate process took until 2 a.m., March 20. Once these three sections were set in place, it took another eight hours to complete the final alignment and joining of the fuselage. The horizontal stabilizer was then installed, as were the landing gear and vertical fin. The procedures established in over six years of 747 production had worked just as well with the new "Junior Jumbo."

Over the next several weeks, final assembly of the Number One SP consisted of completing the aircraft hydraulics, electronics, pressurization, and air conditioning systems. The flight deck instruments were installed at the pilot, co-pilot and flight engineer stations.

Other installation included the engines, APU, inboard flaps, tailcone, dorsal fin, wing-to-body fairings, gear doors, radome, fin, rudder (already painted in the customer's livery so it could be properly balanced prior to installation on the tail fin), and, for certification testing purposes, electronic units for test equipment. In preparation for the big day, the aircraft was tugged across a bridge over a freeway to the massive paint hangar for application of the new red, white and blue SP house colors. On May 7, 1975, Boeing released an announcement that the first Special Performance 747 would be rolled out at 10 a.m. on Monday, May 19, with the initial flight scheduled for July.

The first SP nears completion in March 1975. The aft cargo door shows the framework which supports the lightweight fiberglass fairing. The two full-size 747s in the background had recently returned to Boeing for refurbishment. Air Zaire N747QC (747-121, ln 2/msn 19639) would resume service as Pan Am N747PA *Clipper America*. Boeing purchased Delta Air Lines' N9898 (747-132, ln 94/msn 19898) and leased it back to China Airlines as B-1860. (The Boeing Company)

Rollout

Thousands of employees and guests assembled for the big moment broke into applause as the new jet, wearing Pan American registration N530PA, was rolled out of the factory and onto the apron. RA001, the first full-size 747 (ln 1/msn 20235), was parked nearby to provide scale for its smaller cousin, the 265th 747. Dignitaries gave speeches lavishing praise on the new SP. Kenneth F. Holtby, Boeing Commercial Airplane Company Vice President and 747 Division General Manager, described the SP as "a real winner," the first product of a project in which "everything has been on the plus side. It has been produced within budget and ahead of schedule, and we confidently predict its performance in flight will meet or exceed expectations." John M. Wolgast, Pan Am Senior Vice President-Technical Operations, termed the SP the "epitome of subsonic airliners and we think it will remain supreme probably forever in its class." Representing other airlines purchasing the SP were J.G.H. Loubser, Director General-Transportation Services for the government of South Africa, and Captain "Pie" Pienaar, Chief Executive of South African Airways. Iran Air was represented by Hushang Tajadod, Senior Deputy Managing Director for Corporate Planning.

All involved in the rollout ceremony had a huge stake in this revolutionary new aircraft. Two intense years of design refinements and manufacturing were completed to get to the rollout. Less than two months would bring the SP to the next step: seeing how well it would actually fly.

Rollout of the first "Junior Jumbo" on Monday, May 19, 1975. The aircraft wore its Pan Am registration number (N530PA) for the occasion, later assuming N747SP for first flight and testing. Thousands of Boeing employees, guests and customers watched the spectacle. (The Boeing Company Archives)

Chapter III
FLIGHT TEST

An awesome sight in the July heat. N747SP returns to the runway at Paine Field from her maiden flight. (The Boeing Company)

An energetic program of engineering tests was planned for the 747SP, leading up to U.S. Federal Aviation Administration certification. The first three aircraft off the production line, N747SP (ln 265/msn 21022), N247SP (ln 268/msn 21023), and N347SP (ln 270/msn 21024), would be specially equipped for this program. N747SP was fitted with extensive sophisticated electronic equipment required to record and process flight test data. After its first flight in July 1975, plans were made for the aircraft to complete initial investigation of stability and control, stalls, wing flap loads and deflections, and low-speed airplane drag tests during its first month of flight. Flight flutter, ground braking, and low- and high-speed airspeed calibration tests were also scheduled.

N247SP, the second SP, would begin tests in August, with the third (N347SP) following in October. The fourth SP, N40135 (ln 273/msn 21025), completed in November, became a standby airplane to be used if necessary to maintain the testing schedule. The three aircraft were scheduled to fly a total of 365 hours of engineering tests. The original 747 flight test program required a total of 1,440 hours of flying before certification – the difference in hours was due to the SP being a derivative rather than an entirely new model. About 250 Boeing employees were directly involved in the flight test program under the supervision of Director of Flight Test, S.L. "Lew" Wallick. Pilots, flight engineers, flight test engineers, instrumentation specialists, photographers, mechanics, technicians and inspectors would record and interpret the results of the test flights. A new high-speed flight test data system with improved on-board monitoring capability allowed the review of test data in flight. These data could be gathered with a much smaller volume of equipment aboard the aircraft. Ten racks of equipment were required on each test airplane, compared with 20 on the original 747; only three operators were required, compared to four on the test airplanes in the 1969 trials.

Numerous unseen measuring devices were incorporated into the flight test aircraft: strain gauges to measure structural loads, temperature and pressure pickups, and accelerometers to measure vibrations and vibration-damping. Test equipment more easily seen included retractable trailing cones at the tip of the vertical fin and at the end of the fuselage. These were used during flight tests to trail in error-free static air pressure sources for accurate airspeed measurements. In addition to installation of new equipment in the airplane, other preparations for flight testing the SP included development of a new data processing ground station and computer programs for the flight test data system which provided the recording of 2,000 to 9,000 measurements on a single tape recorder. All of these preparations were put in place by the end of June 1975.

The crew for the first flight of the SP. From left to right: Jack Waddell, pilot; S.L. "Lew" Wallick, co-pilot; and Kenneth R. Storms, flight engineer. Waddell also flew the initial flights of the Boeing 707-320B, -320C, 720B, 737-200, as well as the first 747. (The Boeing Company)

The Flight Crew

The crew chosen to make the first flight of the 747SP had a combined total of 60 years of flight testing experience. The captain for the flight would be Jack Waddell, Boeing Chief Test Pilot. Waddell served as the 747 project pilot since the beginning of the jumbo jet program in 1966 and flew the first flight of the 747 prototype in February 1969. He carried out nearly all flight testing during the original test program, which involved five 747s, and subsequently much of the developmental test flying with the first 747. A Boeing test pilot since 1957, Waddell had been involved with the SP since the aircraft was conceived in the early 1970s, working with the design engineers to ensure that the SP's flight characteristics would be the same as the standard 747s. In the months leading up to the first flight, he evaluated the handling of the new airliner in a special Boeing simulator.

Waddell's flight-test duties for Boeing included work with the B-52 Stratofortress, the KC-135 Stratotanker, and all Boeing commercial jet aircraft programs. He flew the initial flights of the 720B, 707-320B and -320C, 737-200, as well as the 747.

In the right seat of the SP was Lew Wallick, Director of Flight Operations, Boeing Commercial Airplane Company. Until his appointment as Director in June 1974, Wallick served as Senior Engineering Test Pilot. He joined Boeing in 1951 at the company's Wichita (Kansas) plant as an engineer, later transferring to the flight test organization as an experimental test pilot in the B-47 jet bomber program. In 1955 he transferred to the Seattle flight test organization where he served as test pilot in the B-52, KC-135, 707 and 720 test programs. He was pilot for the maiden flight of the fifth 747 during the original flight test program in 1969.

Flight Engineer for the initial flight was Kenneth R. Storms. Storms headed the group of flight engineers involved in test-flying of Boeing jet airliners. He joined The Boeing Company in 1958 as an aerospace engineer, and became associated with the flight-test organization in 1966 as a flight-test engineer, becoming a flight engineer in December of the same year. Storms was involved in experimental test flights of the Boeing 707 and 727 and was project flight engineer on the fifth 747 during the FAA certification program.

Flying the Canadair CF-86 Sabre chase plane was Boeing Engineering Test Pilot, F. Paul Bennett. His job involved both flying new models of Boeing aircraft and observing their characteristics from a chase plane. Bennett joined Boeing in 1960 as an aerodynamic analysis engineer in the company's flight test organization. Later he was operations engineer on the first 727 and KC-135B tanker. Subsequent piloting assignments have involved production testing, engineering testing and training of other pilots on the KC-135, 707, 727, 737 and 747.

The Weigh-In

A satisfying moment for Joseph Sutter, Boeing Commercial Airplane Company Vice President-Program Operations, came when the 747SP weighed in lighter than guaranteed. A friendly $10 wager between Sutter and John G. Borger, Pan American Vice President and Chief Engineer, was made prior to the official determination, which took place on scales built into the floor of the paint hangar. The actual scale weight of the aircraft was 316,358 pounds, less 24,927 pounds of flight test systems and equipment, making the adjusted scale weight a total of 291,431 pounds. Boeing guaranteed the total specification weight to a total of 294,910 pounds. The total difference between the adjusted scale weight and the specification guaranteed weight (worth $10 to Joe Sutter and a great deal more to Pan Am) was 3,479 pounds in Boeing's favor. Though Mr. Borger lost the wager, Pan American won – because for every pound the SP was lighter, a greater number of passengers, larger payload, and more fuel could be carried

Taxi Tests

The final major step before the first flight took place on Sunday, June 29. Four runs were made on the 9,000-foot runway at Paine Field, Everett. These preliminary trials included control responses, ground handling and wheel-brake performance. Test pilot Jack Waddell was satisfied with the results and gave the green light for the first flight.

First Flight

The 747SP's much anticipated first flight came on Independence Day, July 4, 1975. Appropriately painted in patriotic red, white, and blue colors, the SP lifted off the runway at Paine Field, Everctt, at 11:17 a.m., into the clear skies. The flight, later called "by far the most ambitious first flight" of any new Boeing aircraft, lasted 3 hours, 4 minutes, and included the entire normal speed range from full stall to Mach .92. Test pilot Jack Waddell said "a full stall on an initial flight is a rare event." He also said he did not believe "any other airplane had been tested on its first flight to determine the freedom of the airplane's structure from any flutter tendencies, as in the speed runs up to Mach .92." Other tests included airspeed calibration, determination of miles-per-pound of fuel burned, and tests of the new trailing-edge flap system. The flaps were problem-free and exhibited good aerodynamics. During the flight program, the SP was flown over the Pacific Northwest near the Canadian border, reaching a maximum altitude of 30,000 feet and obtaining a top speed of about 630 miles per hour before returning to Paine Field. Later in the day, it took off again and flew an additional 52-minute flight for further engineering tests, landing at Boeing Field, Seattle.

Certification Testing

Confident in the new aircraft and its employees, Boeing established a very brisk pace for the SP's FAA certification test program due for completion by the end of 1975. This schedule was even more impressive when one considers that while the first SP was making its maiden flight on July 4, the second aircraft – having just rolled out the previous week – was on the flight line awaiting its first flight in August, and the third SP was still being built in the factory, not due to fly until October.

Two weeks after the first flight, N747SP had already logged 26 hours during seven test flights, providing a complete

John Borger, Pan American Vice President and Chief Engineer, and Joseph Sutter, Boeing Commercial Airplane Company Vice President-Program Operations, review the numbers from the weigh-in of N747SP. Mr. Sutter is pleased because he just won a friendly $10 wager when the SP came in 3,479 pounds underweight. (The Boeing Company Archives)

With a dramatic shadow caused by the high midday sun, N747SP lifts off from the runway at 11:17 a.m. on July 4, 1975. Photographer By Wingett captured the historic initial flight in a series of photographs taken from the Boeing helicopter. (The Boeing Company)

Four taxi test runs of N747SP (ln 265/msn 21022) were made on Paine Field's 9,000-foot runway six days prior to the maiden flight. Pilot Jack Waddell was at the controls. (The Boeing Company)

"The most ambitious first flight." N747SP over the Olympic Mountains of Washington State, flanked by Boeing's Canadair CF-86 Sabre chase plane. (The Boeing Company)

shakedown of the new aircraft, including stability and control. The structural dynamics tests (which proved the airplane's structure was free of any tendency to flutter) were well under way, and a maximum speed of Mach .98 was attained. On the third flight (July 9) the airplane spent 5 hours, 10 minutes in the air, for tests which included autopilot checks, airspeed calibration, pilot evaluation of Dutch-roll damping characteristics, wind-up turns during which the structure was subjected to 2.5 G's (2.5 times the weight of the aircraft), tests of alternate landing gear and flap extensions, and engine re-starts in flight. Earl V. Chester, FAA Engineering Test Pilot, accompanied the flight and landed the aircraft.

By mid-September, with the second SP added to the test fleet, more than 161 hours were logged during 50 flights. N247SP made its initial flight on August 14 and, in the process, gathered data on engine operations. A week later FAA test pilots were on board observing official certification demonstrations. Milestones achieved at this point included clearance of the airliner as flutter-free to the maximum design Mach number (Mach .97) and maximum design speed (445 knots IAS). All Boeing stall testing had been completed with about 80 stalls carried out at all required weights and center-of-gravity positions. Stall characteristics were described as outstanding. The SP had been flown to 46,000 feet for tests of engine operation and aircraft handling (the rate of climb at that altitude was still 600 feet per minute). The SP was designed to operate in service at a maximum altitude of 45,100 feet. Automatic landings were tested using a dual-channel autopilot. The automatic braking system was able to bring a light-weight SP to a stop in 1,600 feet after landing at Boeing Field. Maximum takeoff weight (MTOW) was 687,000 pounds, well over that at which the SP would initially fly in service. On September 12, N747SP departed for Edwards Air Force Base, California, for certification testing to establish takeoff and landing distances.

On December 22, 1975, Boeing announced that the three-plane fleet of 747SPs had completed test flying for FAA certification two weeks ahead of schedule. A total of 544 hours, 27 minutes were logged on 340 flights during the test program. These figures did not include the 140 hours of time flown by the number four SP (N40135, ln 273/msn 21025) during its worldwide demonstration tour. Lew Wallick called the test program "highly successful," incurring no major problems with the airplanes, engines or equipment. FAA pilots participated in the testing throughout the program beginning with the SP's third flight. Aircraft One (N747SP) and Three (N347SP) were returned to the Everett factory for refurbishment in preparation for delivery to Pan American. Aircraft Two (N247SP) would remain in test status until mid-May 1976, for post-certification test flying.

Excellent view of the first landing of N747SP. (The Boeing Company)

Type Certificate Awarded

Dr. John L. McLucas, administrator of the U.S. Federal Aviation Administration presented the Boeing 747SP its type certificate on February 4, 1976. Receipt of the certificate granted full approval for the aircraft to enter commercial service. The award was made to T.A. Wilson, Boeing Chairman and Chief Executive Officer, at the 747 Division plant in Everett. In awarding the certificate, Dr. McLucas called attention to the cooperation between the FAA and Boeing which helped facilitate the certification process. He said the award "recognizes the achievement on the part of The Boeing Company of another milestone in bringing to the market an airplane which will make significant advances in civil air transportation." The first delivery of the Special Performance 747 was made to Pan American one month later, on March 5, 1976.

Above: T.A. Wilson, Boeing Board Chairman (center), and William M. Allen, Chairman Emeritus (right), congratulate pilot Jack Waddell, after the successful 3-hour, 4-minute initial flight of N747SP. (The Boeing Company)

Left: Kegs of water in the aft cargo bay serve as ballast during flight testing. Scores of these kegs serve to represent the weight of a full or partial load of passengers, luggage, or cargo. Because of the reductions in the length of the aft fuselage section, part of the fiberglass honeycomb wing-to-body fairing is attached to the full-size cargo door. Note rollout registration N530PA still applied to the aircraft. (The Boeing Company Archives)

Takeoff and landing distances for certification were tested at Edwards Air Force Base, California, in September 1975. The attachment on the aft fuselage allows the Number One aircraft (N747SP) to be held at the rotation point for an extended period. Smoke rises from a wooden plank which burns as it scrapes the surface of the runway. (The Boeing Company Archives)

First Flight Postal Cover

Postal cachet carried aboard the first flight of the 747SP. Inside the envelope was a color postcard featuring a photograph of the SP at rollout, parked next to the first 747. The reverse side of the postcard provided statistics on the new aircraft and the following statement: "This envelope with its commemorative cachet was carried on the initial flight of the first Boeing 747SP (Special Performance) airliner. The new airplane took off from Paine Field, adjacent to the Boeing 747 Division plant at Everett, Washington, about 26 miles (42 km) north of Seattle, on the date and at the time shown on the envelope postmark." The souvenir cachets were priced at 25 cents each and could be ordered by Boeing employees through an address listed in the Boeing News. (Author's Collection)

Chapter IV
747/747SP Comparison

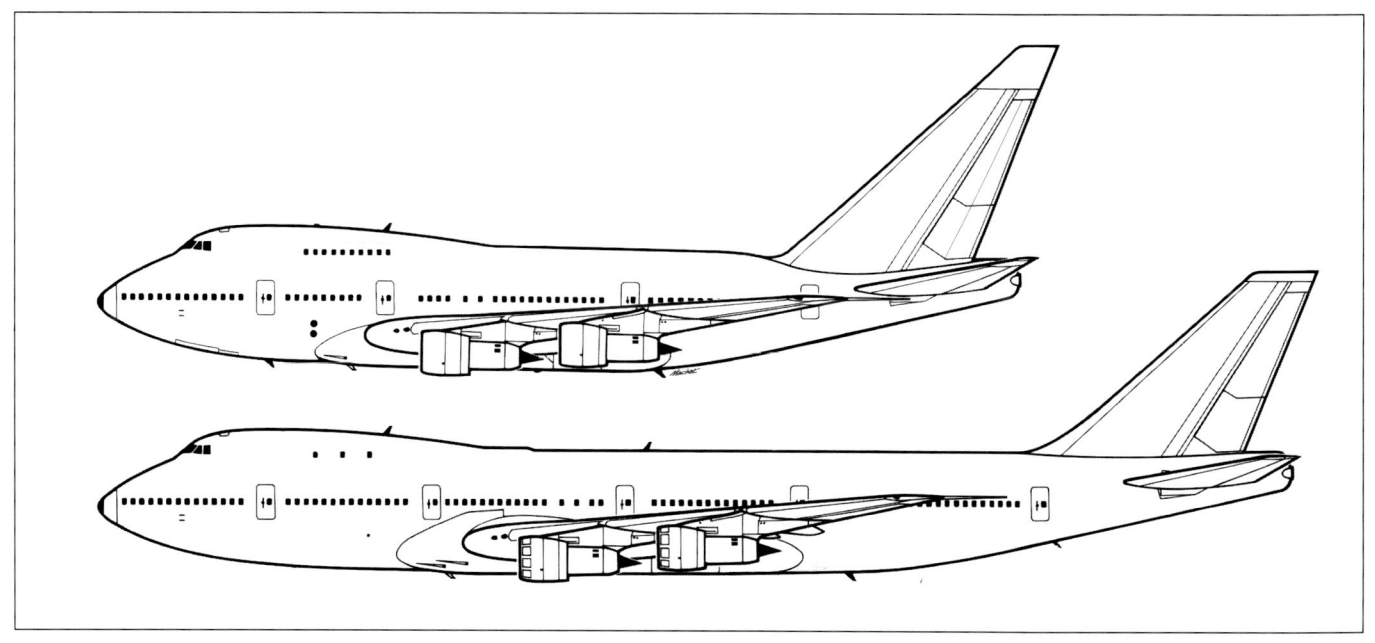

What a difference 48 feet can make. A comparison of size between the SP and the original 747. Both aircraft drawings are rendered in the same scale. (Courtesy of Mike Machat)

Commonality

The 747SP was designed to serve markets of longer ranges and/or lower densities than routes flown by the full-size 747, while maintaining profitability and the 747 standard of space and comfort. In addition to its range and performance capabilities, another selling point for the 747SP was its high degree of commonality with the other members of the 747 family. Since it was a derivative of the 747-100 rather than an entirely new type, the SP retained approximately 92 percent of the original structure, as well as the 747's reliability, maintainability and handling characteristics. Because of this commonality, the cost of placing the SP into the fleet of an airline operating 747s was also much less than required for introduction of an entirely new aircraft type.

Airlines watching the bottom line appreciated the fact that, of the 797 line replaceable units or LRUs (items that can be repaired or replaced on the flight line), 700 – or 88 percent – were common with the 747. Air conditioning and pressurization systems, communications equipment, hydraulic power, ice and rain protection, instruments, lights, oxygen systems, pneumatics, the auxiliary power unit and windows are completely interchangeable. Full commonality also applies to numerous engine components – including fuel and oil systems, controls, indicating and starting systems – if the airline selected the identical power plant for its 747 fleet. Half of the remaining 97 uncommon items are associated with either the landing gear or the flight controls. The landing gear changes were made to reduce weight and changes in the flight controls were made to match the handling of the full-size 747.

These same flight characteristics were confirmed by both the manufacturer and several airlines. According to Boeing, from the perspective of the flight crew, the SP was completely interchangeable with the 747-100 and 200. Boeing documents indicate that only a "four- to seven-hour" training period was required to familiarize 747 cockpit crews. Pan Am reported that their pilot transition consisted of "one hour of ground school, no check ride, and no simulator." South African 747 crews were given "a one-day 'differences' course and one hour's flying in the 747SP before commencing line operations." To acquaint their 747-trained cabin crews, airlines flying the SP needed only to provide a half-day differences course. Crew training equipment, materials and instructors, as well as crew dispatcher training would also be the same for mixed 747 fleets.

Fuselage

To build the SP, the 747-100 fuselage was reduced by 48 feet, 4 inches – to 176 feet, 9 inches – giving the aircraft its unmistakably chubby appearance. When compared to the 747-100, the SP's overall length (from nose to tail) is shorter by just 47 feet, to 184 feet, 9 inches total. The difference between the fuselage length and the overall length takes into account the adjustments made to the tail section of the SP's fuselage and the extended length of the SP vertical fin. To accommodate these structural changes, three of the five 747 main body sections required major modifications.

Section 41, at 35 feet, 9 inches, is identical on both models, extending from the tip of the radome to one window past the Number One entry door. Section 42 was reduced by 16 feet, 8 inches, to a total length of 23 feet, 4 inches. This section required substantial modification to accommodate placement of the Number Two entry door. On the full size 747, Section 42 ends as the slope of the upper deck meets the main fuselage. On the SP, this section ends about two-thirds of the way down this slope, one window past the Number Two entry door. Section 44 was changed to incorporate the remainder of the upper deck, however, the overall length of 40 feet for this section is the same as the original.

19

747SP General Arrangement

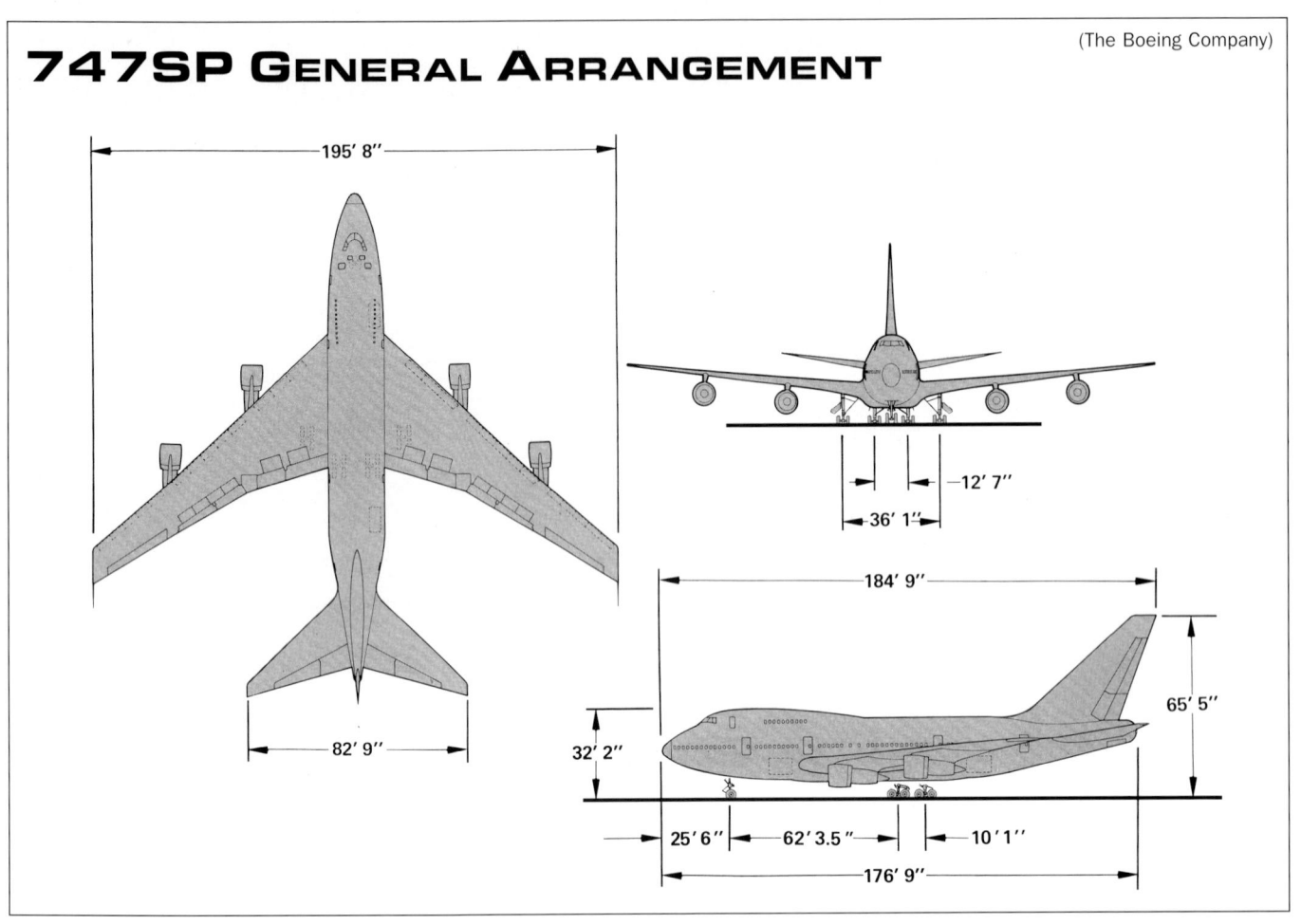

(The Boeing Company)

- 195' 8"
- 82' 9"
- 12' 7"
- 36' 1"
- 184' 9"
- 65' 5"
- 32' 2"
- 25' 6"
- 62' 3.5"
- 10' 1"
- 176' 9"

747-100B/-200B General Arrangement

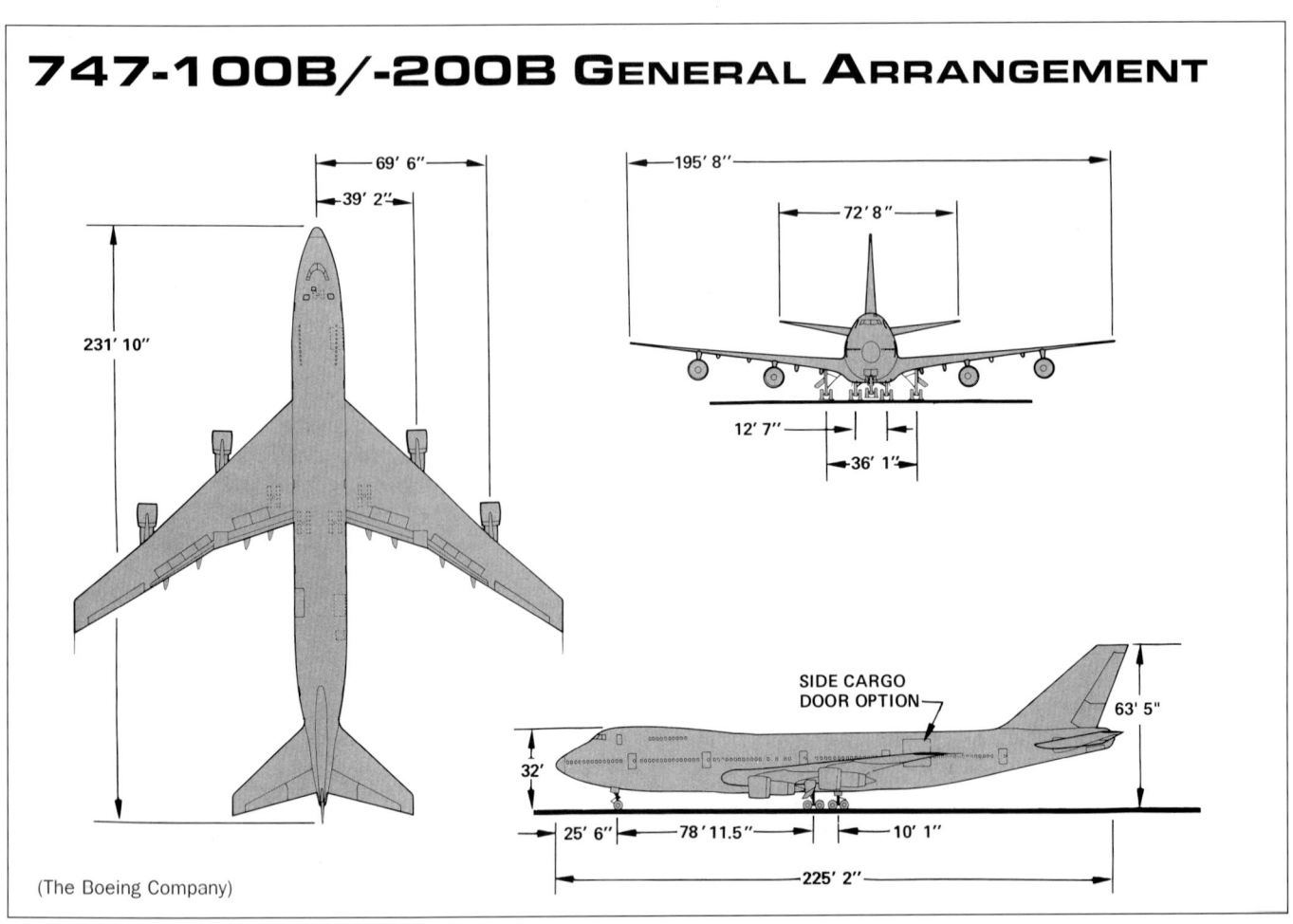

- 69' 6"
- 39' 2"
- 231' 10"
- 195' 8"
- 72' 8"
- 12' 7"
- 36' 1"
- SIDE CARGO DOOR OPTION
- 63' 5"
- 32'
- 25' 6"
- 78' 11.5"
- 10' 1"
- 225' 2"

(The Boeing Company)

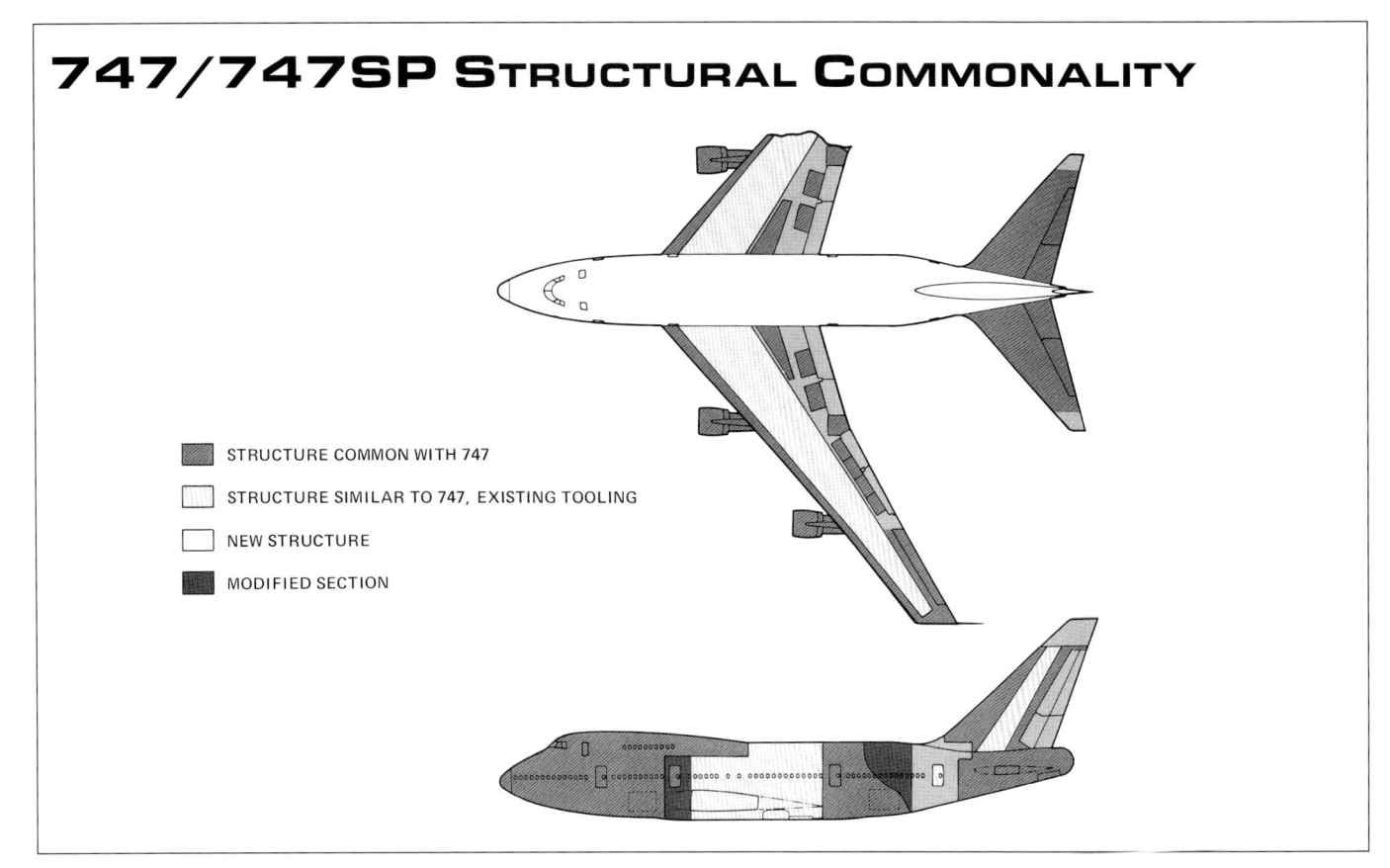

747/747SP Structural Commonality

- STRUCTURE COMMON WITH 747
- STRUCTURE SIMILAR TO 747, EXISTING TOOLING
- NEW STRUCTURE
- MODIFIED SECTION

This graphic illustrates which SP structures were common with the 747, structures similar enough to be built with existing 747 tooling, and which were new structures exclusive to the SP. The assembly photograph on page 10 shows how these changes were incorporated into the five main fuselage sections. (The Boeing Company)

Manufacturing of Section 44 was completed using existing tooling. Reductions, modifications, and entirely new structures were incorporated into the 41-feet, 8-inch-long Section 46. Because this section was reduced by a hefty 31 feet, 8 inches, the aft end needed to be recontoured to join with the unchanged tail section (Section 48) which measured 36 feet in length. These reductions left the SP with four main entry doors on each side, compared to five on the 747. The redesign of the fuselage also required incorporating a new wing/fuselage fairing, which is the largest single fiberglass molding used on an aircraft.

Empennage

In order to maintain the same handling and control characteristics as the original 747, changes were made to the empennage (tail section) of the SP. The height of the huge (886-square-foot) vertical fin was increased by 5 feet, and the horizontal stabilizer is 10 feet wider. A double-hinged rudder design, which increases effectiveness and allows control equal to the standard 747, was unique to the SP (the rudder area of the SP is the same). The vertical fin structure was strengthened to accept the increased loads resulting from the revised rudder design. Due to the changes made in the aft-fuselage section, the dorsal was also reshaped.

The SP fin, rudder and fuselage Section 48 were positioned 38 inches lower to the ground than the same section and fin on the standard 747. Section 48 was also rotated up 1 degree. As a result of these changes, and even though the fin tip of the SP had been extended 5 feet, it was actually only 2 feet higher than the tail of the standard 747.

Wing

The wing span for the SP is identical to the larger 747-100/200B models, at 195 feet, 8 inches, and the wing planform for the 747SP is also essentially the same as the larger models. Reductions in takeoff and landing weights permitted incorporation of a new variable-pivot flap design in place of the 747 triple-slotted flap. Because of the new design, the SP lacks the large track fairing pods of the full-size aircraft. When retracted, the single-slotted trailing-edge flaps are nested in a similar fashion as the triple-slotted flaps on the full-size aircraft. This new design provided a much simpler and lighter trailing-edge flap system while providing good lift characteristics for takeoff and landing.

Changes were made to the wing box both for the flap support system and to reduce weight. The structure weight for the wing was decreased by reducing the gauges of spars, ribs, skin and stringers in the wing box section. Power sources for the control surfaces, as well as fueling, de-fueling and fuel jettison systems are identical to the original 747. The SP's fuel containment system is identical to the 747. This system has seven integral tanks and a fuel capacity of 48,783 U.S. gallons (compared to 47,331 gallons in the -100), and an optional configuration which expands the total capacity to 50,359 U.S. gallons. Like the 747-100, all fuel is stored in two outboard main tanks, two inboard main tanks, two reserve tanks and a center wing structure within the fuselage.

Weight

With the many weight reductions made in the wing, fuselage, and landing gear, the SP was substantially lighter than the other 747

The SP's double-hinge rudder is clearly shown in this comparison between tails of the SP pictured on the left (N530PA), and the standard 747. The 5 feet added to the SP tail fin can be seen in the distance from the top of the rudder to the top of the fin. The retractable trailing cones used in flight test, and the APU exhaust port are also visible. (The Boeing Company Archives)

types. The basic 747SP was offered at a maximum gross takeoff weight of 660,000 pounds. Five other gross-weight options were available, ranging from a minimum of 630,000 to a maximum of 700,000 pounds (this range option varied from 710,000 to 735,000 pounds on the 747-100). The maximum landing weight of the SP was set at 450,000 pounds, and the zero fuel weight became 410,000 pounds.

Engine Options

A wide range of engines permitted selections that satisfied the particular performance and commonality requirements of the operators. The standard engine offered to customers was the Pratt and Whitney JT9D-7A, with 46,950 pounds of thrust. The Pratt and Whitney engines were the most popular, with 39 of the 45 SPs built using this type. Several different models of the JT9D were offered, with takeoff thrust varying from 46,950 up to 50,000 pounds. General Electric's CF6 and the Rolls Royce RB.211-524 engines were also available as options. The Rolls Royce examples were the most powerful available for the SP, offering up to 51,600 pounds of thrust. RB.211-524 engines, available since mid-1976, were installed on a total of six aircraft. General Electric engines were not selected to power any of the 747SP aircraft. Boeing offered a total of 54 different combinations of engine and gross-weight options.

The 747SP auxiliary power unit (APU) is identical to that of the 747-100, incorporating a 1,100-horsepower axial flow gas turbine and one generator. A second generator was optional. Using fuel from the number two main tank, the APU provides engine starts, air conditioning, electric power and hydraulic-pump drive during airport operations without ground power units.

Cargo

In the basic configuration, the SP has a lower deck cargo capacity of 20 LD-1 half-width containers, compared to 30 on the standard 747. Each LD-1 container could carry up to 173 cubic feet of cargo, and measured 92 inches wide, 60.4 inches long, and 64 inches high. The SP has a total of 3,460 cubic feet of lower deck container cargo space available, plus 400 cubic feet of additional bulk cargo space, versus room for 6,250 cubic feet of container cargo and 1,000 cubic feet of bulk cargo on the 747. Many different types of pallets and containers can be accommodated in the lower holds. The two 66-inch-high by 104-inch-wide lower deck cargo doors are identical in size to the 747s. All standard unit loading devices can be used with the SP.

Airplane Systems and Options

A ground proximity warning system (GPWS) and an advanced braking system, available as options on the full size 747, were included as standard equipment on all 747SPs. The GPWS makes use of the airliner's radio altimeter and barometric altitude indication, as well as an on-board computer, to prevent inadvertent descent below safe altitudes. When conditions warrant, the system warning lights illuminate on both the pilot's and co-pilot's instrument panels and a voice warns the pilots to "pull up."

The auto-brake system automatically applies the brakes after touchdown and maintains constant deceleration which results in reduced stopping distances and greater passenger comfort. The pilot can override the system at any time. Should the pilot decide to take off again immediately after touching down, the auto-brake system switches off as soon as the throttles are advanced. An anti-skid feature is operative whether the auto-brake system is used or not. A benefit of the system is improved brake and tire life.

In 1975, the 747 and 747SP aircraft were approved by the Federal Aviation Administration to carry up to 32 passengers plus crew in the upper deck. The SP had originally been certified to carry 16 passengers upstairs (early 747s could only carry eight passengers in the upper deck until an improved escape slide and stairway smoke barrier were approved in 1971). To enable the 747 to carry additional passengers, a port-side upper deck emergency exit was installed just aft of the cockpit, opposite of the emergency exit installed in all 747s. Both exits were fitted with an emergency slide. Aircraft already delivered could be modified by Boeing to incorporate this feature.

A new straightened stairway design to permit easier access to the upper deck was made available in February 1976. The stairway could be ordered as an option in newly ordered 747s or retrofitted in those already in service. The new stairs are located in about the same position as the spiral stairs and consists of two flights of steps, arranged in an L-shape.

The 747 prototype is shown here with its massive triple-slotted flaps fully extended. The large pods under the wing are the flap track fairings which are not required with the SP's simplified system. The immense size of the 747 is highlighted by the scale of the men working below the wing. (Museum of Flight Archives)

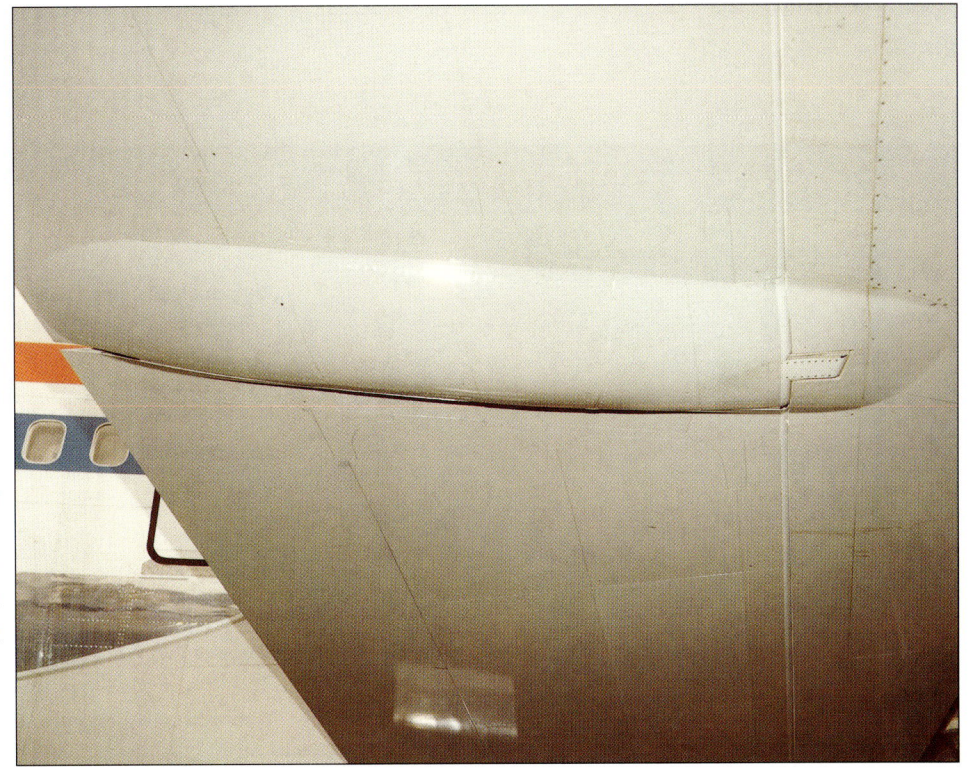

In contrast to the 747's huge flap track fairings, the SP flap mechanism is contained in these relatively modest housings under the wing. (The Boeing Company Archives)

Reduced takeoff and landing weights allowed the use of a new trailing-edge flap design for the SP. The large, variable pivot flap utilized a single segment, rather than the triple-slotted type used on the full-size 747. This photo shows the SP's flaps fully extended. (The Boeing Company Archives)

COMPARISON FIGURES – 747-100 AND 747SP*

	747-100	747SP
Wing Span	195'8"	195'8"
Wing Area (square feet)	5,500	5,500
Wing Sweep (degree)	37.5	37.5
Horizontal Stabilizer Span	72'8"	82'9"
Overall Length (nose to tail)	231'10"	184'9"
Fuselage Length (actual length of fuselage)	225'2"	176'9"
Height	63'5"	65'5"
Tread (distance between outboard main landing gear)	36'1"	36'1"
Cabin Length	187'	138'8"
Cabin Volume (cubic feet)	29,570	22,370
Maximum Width	241.5"	241.5"
Floor Width	233"	233"
Typical Seating Capacity (two-cabin layout)	48/337	28/303
Cargo Volume–all passenger (cubic feet)	6,250	3,460

	747-100	747SP
Number of LD-1 containers + additional bulk cargo	30/1,000 cu-ft	20/400 cu-ft
Standard Engines	4 P&W	4 P&W
Model Designation (basic type, others optional)	JT9D-7A	JT9D-7A
Takeoff Thrust (pounds)	46,950	46,950
Engine Weight (pounds)	8,800	8,800
Fuel Capacity (U.S. gallons)	47,331	48,783
Optional Capacity (U.S. gallons)		50,359
WEIGHT OPTIONS FOR MINIMUM/MAXIMUM CONFIGURATIONS		
Maximum Taxi Weight (pounds)	713,000/ 783,000	636,000/ 703,000
Takeoff Weight (pounds)	710,000/ 735,000	630,000/ 700,000
Landing Weight (pounds)	564,000	450,000
Zero-Fuel Weight (pounds)	526,500	410,000
Typical Airline Operating Empty Weight (pounds)	356,900/ 357,100	330,400/ 331,000
Payload (pounds)	169,600/ 169,400	79,600/ 79,000

* Figures courtesy of The Boeing Company

The SP's light-weight trailing-edge flap system (shown above) provides a cleaner wing surface without the 747's massive flap track fairings (below). (The Boeing Company Archives)

The strut and nacelle of the 747SP (pictured left) were modified to a new configuration which differs dramatically from the full-size 747 (right). The difference in the fuselage length is apparent by looking at the position of the aft cargo door in relationship to the wing-to-body fairing. (The Boeing Company Archives)

25

Chapter V
MARKETING THE 747SP

Artist's concept of a very striking 747SP for Ecuatoriana Airlines of Ecuador. Despite the best efforts of the sales staff, Boeing did not sell a single SP in the South American market. Sales proposals were accompanied with paintings like these, or with retouched photographs, to show just how nice the new aircraft would look in the potential customer's livery. (The Boeing Company Archives)

In the early '70s, Boeing commercial aircraft sales to overseas customers were given the highest priority. Around the world long-range, narrow-body jets were aging and fast becoming due for replacement; the 747 was too big for many markets; the competition was producing high-quality wide-body products, and oil shortages and embargoes were pinching the airlines. Into this scenario came the 747SP, an airplane salesman's dream. It was an innovative, well-built, economical, high-performance aircraft that could fly substantial loads of passengers and cargo in and out of just about any jet-capable airport. Worldwide operators like Pan American embraced the SP enthusiastically and inaugurated new routes all over the globe. It was exactly what operators from distant regions like Asia, Australia, the Middle East, and southern Africa needed to connect their countries with Europe and North America. However, it simply may have been too much airplane for smaller markets and routes where the SP's features were not necessary.

The 747SP files at Boeing are filled with might-have-beens. Illustrations show aircraft in the colors of airlines approached by Boeing to consider the merits of the new SP and what it could do for their bottom line and prestige. It was truly an A-to-Z list of airlines from all corners of the world, including: AeroPeru, Ansett, Ariana, BWIA, Delta, East African, El Al, Gulf Air, Iberia, JAT, Japan, Mexicana, Singapore, and Zambia Airways – almost 40 in all. When looking at the varying needs of these airlines, several factors may have been responsible for the lack of interest in the SP:

1. Cost. Early estimates determined the price of a production SP would be about $28 million a copy, including spares (in 1976 dollars). This was a substantial sum of money and out of reach of many of the airlines targeted. The SP also cost more than the competing long-range DC-10-30 (around $26.5 million, including spares).
2. Limited special performance market. Basic, economical transportation was all that most airlines required to fly the majority of their passengers on most of their routes.
3. The standard 747 was constantly improving. Fuel economy and range were steadily reaching SP levels, while retaining the much larger passenger and cargo capacity of the full-size 747.

In hindsight, the well-worn cliché "the right airplane at the wrong time" really doesn't fit with the SP. Timing wasn't the problem. It seems more likely that it was the right airplane for a very specific, limited market.

Battling the Tri-Jets

From the earliest days of the SP concept, Boeing was carefully sizing up the long- and extra-long-range, medium-density markets. To assist with marketing the SP, sales personnel were armed with specially prepared documents like the February 1974 Sales Handbook: 747SP Versus DC-10-30. Meant for in-house use only, the document was filled with graphs, charts, and statistics and listed numerous advantages of the little 747 over the DC-10-30 in just

The McDonnell Douglas DC-10-30 OH-LHB (ln 201/msn 47957). The DC-10-30 and 747SP wide-bodies would compete in the long-range, medium-density markets. (Jon Proctor)

about every possible area: Gross weight, fuel capacity, ability to carry a greater number of passengers in all configurations, a larger cabin for more headroom and overhead stowage space. Cargo space, while potentially larger in the DC-10, was diminished by the tri-jet's need to carry auxiliary fuel for greater range. The SP exceeded the DC-10-30 performance in takeoff, cruise altitude, and landing, while retaining a substantial range advantage. The comparatively larger wing area gave the 747SP performance advantages over the DC-10, and the noise levels were lower with the SP on takeoff and approach. Flying at 41,000 feet, the SP experienced one-third less turbulence than the DC-10 flying at 35,000 feet, and the turbulence experienced by the SP at the higher altitudes would be less intense.

The document went on to provide economic and marketing advantages of flying the 747SP: The SP had a 9- to 12-percent greater revenue potential than the DC-10-30 because of its greater passenger capacity. Its cost-per-seat-mile was 11 percent less than the DC-10. Greater savings were realized in fleet costs for airlines flying both the full-size 747 and the SP. Survey data showed that the 747 was preferred by passengers and travel agents – by a wide margin – over the DC-10. Over 50 percent of travelers could identify the 747, whereas only 15 percent could identify the DC-10, and 59 percent thought the 747 was more technologically advanced compared to 18 percent for the tri-jet. The 747 also scored substantially higher with passengers on comfort, spaciousness and safety. The document even noted the 747's height advantage, which offered the pilot a better overall view of the airport situation. Of course, marketers for McDonnell Douglas had similar documents showing the numerous advantages of the DC-10 over the 747SP.

Sales rhetoric aside, the DC-10 was a very good aircraft that was successful because McDonnell Douglas adapted it to fit into numerous markets, especially with the DC-10-30 in the mid- to long-range, medium-density routes. Lockheed also produced several versions of the L-1011 tri-jet, including the L-1011-500, a shortened variant built for long-range intercontinental routes. Though the SP was somewhat late coming into the market dominated by the DC-10 and L-1011, Boeing knew that the SP could, in many ways, outperform both California-built wide-bodies, and decided that it was time to let the rest of the world know just how good it really was. In true Boeing style, the sales department chose a unique way to prove their point.

Like the SP, the Lockheed L-1011-500 was an extended-range aircraft with a shortened fuselage. This example is Delta N751DA (msn 1166) at Atlanta. (Jerry Stanick)

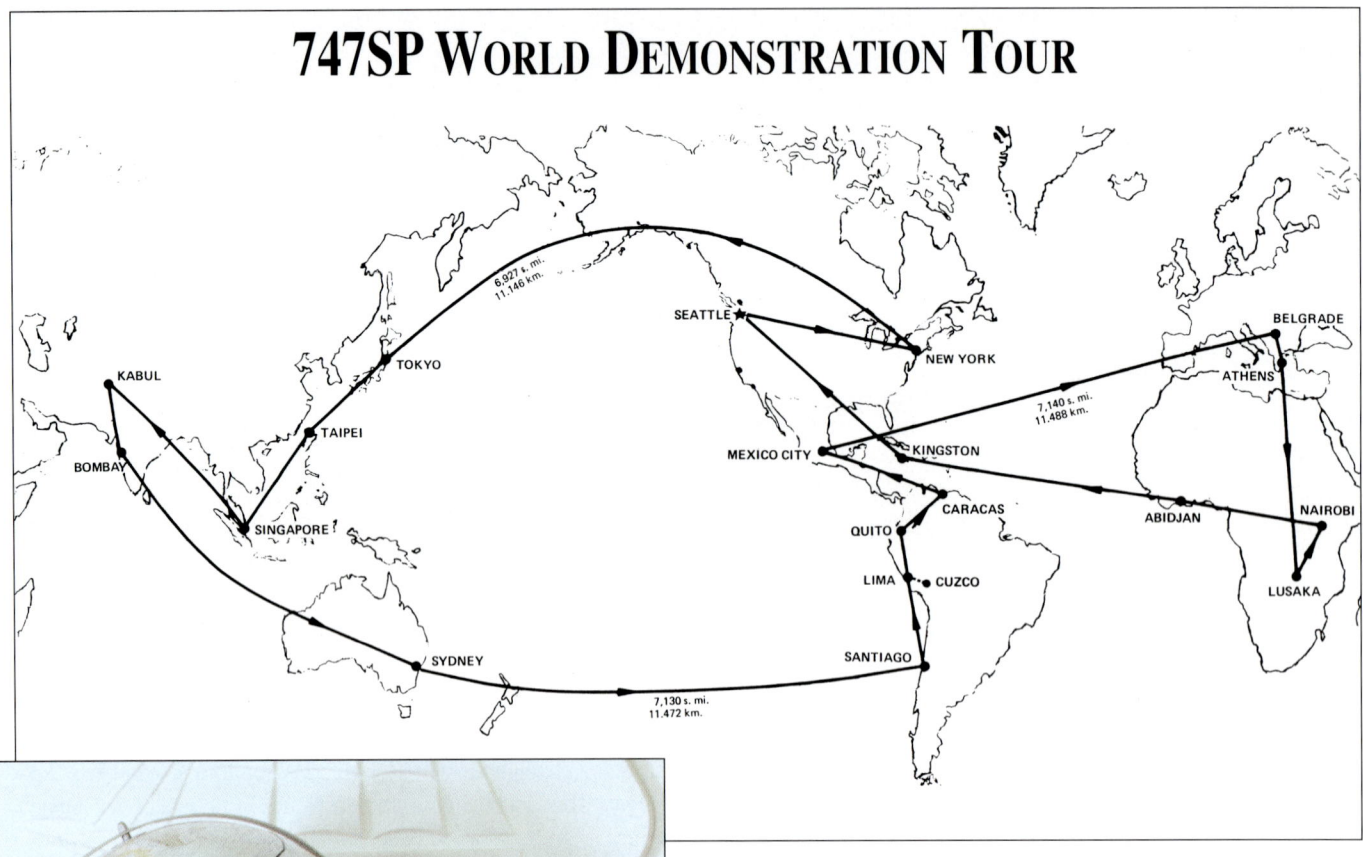

747SP World Demonstration Tour

This map, part of the official Boeing press kit, shows the planned 30-day, 70,000-mile route of the worldwide demonstration tour. The actual route was as shown except for a change which deleted the Lima and Cuzco stops and added La Paz, Bolivia. The actual tour took 29 days and covered 72,152 miles. (The Boeing Company Archives)

A globe onboard shows the extent of the 747SP demonstration tour. While the aircraft did not actually make a complete journey all the way around the earth during the tour, it did fly miles equivalent to three circumnavigations. (The Boeing Company)

747SP World Tour

Boeing was so confident in the abilities of the SP that it took a brand-new aircraft and sent it the equivalent distance of three times around the world in less than a month. N40135 (ln 273/msn 21025) made its maiden flight on November 3, 1975, and eight days later began the 747SP World Tour. It was staged as a 30-day, 70,000-mile demonstration flight, with plans to visit 19 cities in 18 countries and show off the SP's high performance capabilities. The actual tour visited 18 cities and took 29 days, and covered 72,152 miles. The cities of Lima and Cuzco, Peru, were originally on the itinerary but had to be dropped in favor of LaPaz, Bolivia. Marked in the same red, white, and blue as the first SP, N40135 set several speed and distance records along the way.

The aircraft, fitted with a complete Pan American interior, departed from Boeing Field in Seattle at 5:58 a.m. on November 11, bound for New York. The following day, it flew 200 passengers aboard the first nonstop commercial flight from New York to Tokyo – a distance of 7,015 miles – in 13 hours, 33 minutes. From Tokyo the SP visited Taipei; Singapore; Kabul, Afghanistan (becoming the first wide-body aircraft to land at the 5,841-foot-high airport); Bombay; and Sydney. From Sydney, it flew 7,143 miles to Santiago, Chile in 12 hours, 14 minutes, then to the highest airport of the tour, 13,354 feet, at LaPaz, Bolivia. The SP performed flawlessly, using less than 4,000 feet of runway to land. A few minutes later, with 156 guests aboard, it took off, needing only 7,000 feet of runway. Next it was on to Quito, Ecuador (altitude 9,229 feet); and Caracas, Venezuela; then Mexico City. The longest segment of the trip would be flown from Mexico City to Belgrade, Yugoslavia, a total of 7,205 miles, in 12 hours, 56 minutes – the first jet transport to fly nonstop from Mexico City to Europe. The 631,000-pound SP departed from the 7,341-foot-high airport at Mexico City in 75-degree weather. Yugoslavia was left behind for Athens; Lusaka, Zambia; Nairobi, Kenya; and Abidjan, the capital of the Ivory Coast. The final two legs were from Abidjan to Kingston, Jamaica, and back home to Seattle.

During the tour, which took a total of 140 hours, 15 minutes to complete, the aircraft crossed both the North and South Pacific, the

Indian Ocean, and spanned the Atlantic twice. The SP crossed the equator four times, and the International Date Line twice. Highest altitude attained during the flight was 45,000 feet, and four of the nonstop legs were over 6,400 miles in length. The SPs performance was not only shown by the length of the routes it flew, but also by its ability to climb. At Taiwan, the aircraft with 137 passengers aboard, lifted off the runway in less than 3,000 feet. Departing Nairobi, the SP climbed to 45,000 feet in only 20 minutes. More than 2,300 guests were carried during the SP's 20 demonstration flights. Despite the grueling schedule, the only problem with the aircraft was a difficult auxiliary power unit which required repair in Mexico City and again in Kingston, Jamaica. Maintenance was completed by Boeing pre-flight personnel who traveled with the aircraft. The SP never missed a scheduled departure during the entire trip. Not bad for a airplane which started the tour with only 15 hours of total flying time.

N40135 at Abidjan, Ivory Coast, one of three stops in Africa. Ivory Coast President, Felix Houphouet-Boigny, was the highest ranking government official to visit the airplane during the world tour. (The Boeing Company)

Japan Air Lines executives being briefed on the benefits of the SP during the first nonstop commercial jet flight from New York to Tokyo. The complete Pan American interior was installed on N40135 (ln 273/msn 21025) for the flight. (The Boeing Company)

The SP was the main attraction wherever it went during the tour. Chilean soldiers parade past N40135 at the Santiago airport. (The Boeing Company)

29

The final stop of the tour at Kingston, Jamaica. Repairs were made to an auxiliary power unit here and previously in Mexico City – the only mechanical problem encountered during the entire trip. The very tired world tour staff anticipated the final leg of the journey, a nonstop flight home to Seattle. (The Boeing Company)

Modular display panels installed in Zone B. The backlit exhibit provided information on performance, range and features of the SP for guests visiting the aircraft during stops and demonstration flights along the worldwide tour route. (The Boeing Company)

The perfect presidential aircraft. The SP was larger, faster, had a longer range, and was substantially more imposing than the VC-137 (707) aircraft then in use. Presentations extolling these virtues were made; however, the SP never found a place in the government's budget. (The Boeing Company Archives)

VIP Aircraft

Because of its size, speed and range, the SP is the ideal VIP aircraft. When money is no object and one wishes to make a lasting impression, nothing beats rolling up on the tarmac in a private 747. Without a doubt, the SP is the jumbo jet of choice with leaders throughout the Middle East and Asia. Three of the original 45 aircraft were built specifically for VIPs, and another nine SPs, formerly in airline service, were later modified for VIP duties. The rulers of Abu Dhabi, Brunei, Dubai, Iraq, Kazakstan, Oman, Qatar, and Saudi Arabia have or have had these lavishly appointed aircraft at their disposal, and more deluxe SP "flying palaces" are likely to be converted in the future.

In 1977, a detailed proposal was made by Boeing (pages 34-40) to build an aircraft exclusively for the use of His Majesty, the Shah of Iran. The SP would be equipped with necessities to rule his country from anywhere in the world; a complete communications center was included, plus offices, conference areas, and a large dining room. He would also enjoy many of the comforts of home, such as an Imperial Suite with a bedroom, a dressing room and shower. Though it never was ordered, Boeing used the experience gained with this proposal to prepare for others. In 1982, the 747SP was offered as a replacement for the VC-137 (707) aircraft used by the President of the United States. Though the SP had impressive performance, it was simply not large enough for the growing requirements of a future Air Force One. The U.S. government later ordered two 747-2G4Bs – serial numbers 82-8000 and 92-9000, (ln 679/msn 23824 and ln 685/msn 23825) – as VC-25A presidential aircraft.

One of the most impressive and luxurious aircraft ever built was the personal 747SP for His Majesty King Khaled of Saudi Arabia. HZ-HM1 (ln 329/msn 21652) was a flying palace and hospital for the King, who suffered from a heart ailment and required a pacemaker. The King's personal physician was located in Cleveland, Ohio, a long journey from Saudi Arabia in case of complications. A fully equipped hospital with operating room was installed on board. In case of emergency, the King's stateroom was equipped with a defibrillator. Some of the many fine furnishings included a complete sound and multi-screen video system, cabin panels covered in silk, and thick wool carpeting throughout the aircraft. First-class-style seating was covered in rich fabrics; telephones with silver handsets nested in walnut chests; and lavatories included controls for music and special lighting. Details included the royal crest on the seatbelt buckles and cabin doors. An amazing aircraft, it was superseded when King Fahd succeeded King Khaled and had an even more luxurious 747-3G1 (HZ-HM1A, ln 592/msn 23070) built as his personal aircraft. The SP's registration was then changed to HZ-HM1B. The Saudi Royal Flight aircraft were painted in the same colors as the Saudia airliners, without the titles on the tail fin. This aircraft has recently been repainted in the new Saudi Arabian sand and white livery with a royal blue tail fin. A second SP HZ-AIJ (ln 560 /msn 22750) was transferred from Saudia service to Royal Flight duties in 1992.

The second of the VIP SPs built by Boeing was YI-ALM (ln 567/msn 22858) for Iraq. Ordered by Iraqi Airways, the aircraft was immediately transferred to the Iraqi government upon delivery on August 30, 1982. Similar in layout to the proposal submitted to the Shah of Iran (see page 34), the furnishings are more practical and not as plush as many of the other VIP SPs in the region. This aircraft features a bedroom with two chairs and a small round table, plus an informal office area in Zone A. Zone B has 16 airline-style first-class seats in rows along the windows, plus six swivel/sleeper chairs and two tables in a center lounge area. These seats are all covered in a red velvet-like cloth, as are 16 first-class seats on the upper deck. The forward half of Zone C features a conference room (pictured on the next page). Staff seating is in a standard three-four-three coach-class arrangement throughout the aft portion of Zones C and D. The aircraft was grounded in Tozeur, Tunisia, during the Gulf War, where it remains today because of the Iraqi no-fly restrictions. Formerly in the Iraqi Airways green livery (with Iraq titles), YI-ALM is now painted all white with no titles.

The 45th and final SP built (A6-ZSN, ln 676/msn 23610) was specially ordered by the government of Abu Dhabi – almost four years after the 44th (YI-ALM) was delivered. The SP rolled out only nine months after the order was placed, but it took almost another three years to deliver after installation of luxurious furnishings and a communications center.

Glass Cockpit

Originally delivered to Trans World Airlines, A6-SMR (ln 415/msn 21961) is one of several 747SPs refurbished for use as a VIP aircraft. Obtained by the Government of Dubai in 1985, this particular example is the first (and so far, only) 747SP to receive a modernized "glass cockpit" conversion, heretofore seen only on 747-400 models. Lufthansa Technik completed the project at its Hamburg facility. (Andrew Cline)

Above: Deluxe first-class guest seating in Saudi Royal Flight HZ-HM1 (ln 329/msn 21652). The aircraft was designed for the exclusive use of King Khaled and the royal family and is lavishly furnished throughout. The aircraft was re-registered HZ-HM1B when an even more luxurious 747-300 was built for King Fahd. (Boeing Commercial Airplane Group)

Below: Conference room aboard the Iraqi Government 747SP YI-ALM (ln 567/msn 22858). This room featured seating for 15 around the large table and in seats along the right side cabin wall. The aircraft also boasted a bedroom, office work space and a forward cabin with an informal conference area. (The Boeing Company Archives)

The following seven pages are condensed from a deluxe presentation brochure published by The Boeing Company for the Shah of Iran. The December 1977 proposal was covered in royal blue leatherette with gold lettering, parchment end pages and a fold-out of the cabin layout. The original publication featured each illustration on a full page with the corresponding text opposite. (Museum of Flight Archives)

Imperial Iranian Air Force 1

The Boeing 747SP Executive Airplane for His Imperial Majesty

The Boeing 747SP described in this proposal for His Imperial Majesty is the most advanced executive jet airplane in the world.

The capabilities of the airplane itself offer His Imperial Majesty global reach – the capital cities of nations around the world are within nonstop range.

Within a matter of hours, His Imperial Majesty can be anywhere on earth he chooses.

At the same time, a highly sophisticated communications package allows continuous contact with Niavaron Palace and links the National Executive Authority with military and civilian networks.

The ship is an airborne extension of His Imperial Majesty's sovereign territory – a means to address sensitive international issues on a personal and timely basis, without turning away from urgent domestic matters.

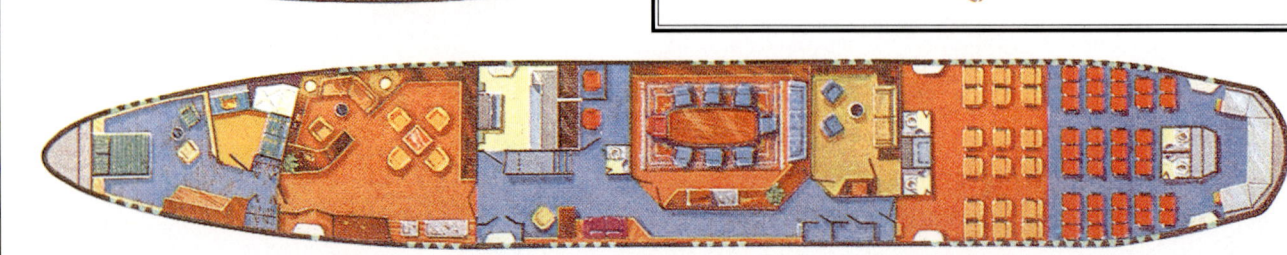

Iran has the infrastructure required for this advanced airplane.

Iran has extensive experience with 747-class airplanes, and was one of the first nations in the world to fly the 747SP after it was certified last year.

The accumulated experience, skills, maintenance facilities, spares and other support capabilities already in place would make the transition to a 747SP executive airplane simple and smooth.

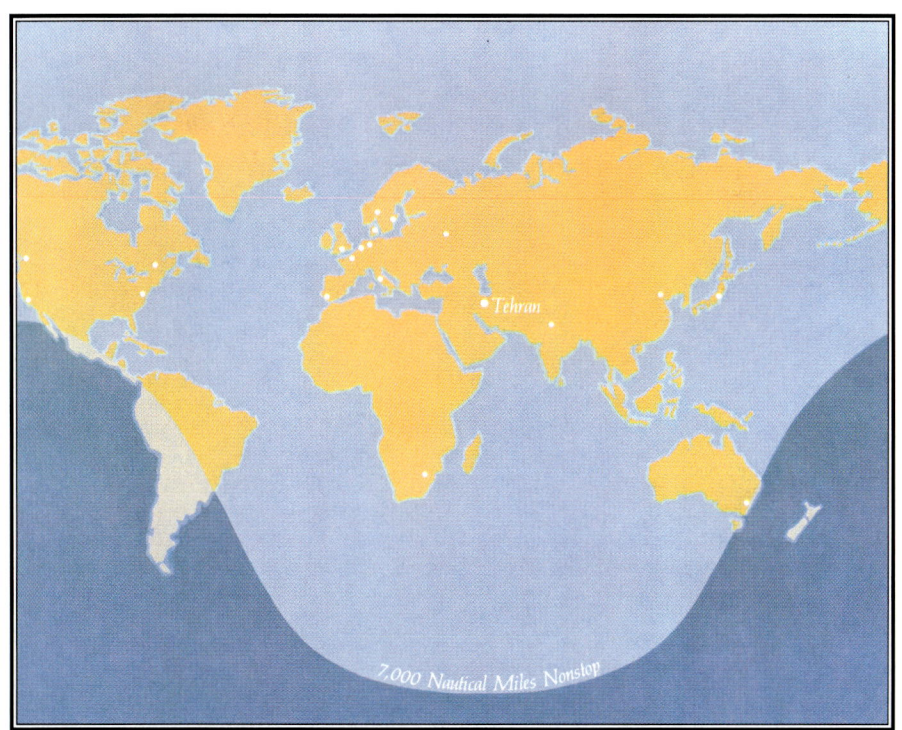

His Imperial Majesty would have the world's longest range executive airplane.

The 747SP is ideally suited to executive service in which the central requirement is an international presence – it can fly higher, cruise faster and has greater range than any other jetliner.

For example, the executive 747SP designed for His Imperial Majesty could fly 7,000 nautical miles, nonstop. On a flight from Tehran to Washington, D.C., the executive airplane would climb to an altitude of 35,000 feet within 30 minutes, cruise comfortably at 501 knots true airspeed, more than 4,000 feet above the relatively crowded commercial air lanes. Flying times would be approximately 13 hours. On a return trip, the 747SP's ability to climb quickly through traffic, and to cruise at 37,000 feet, would mean just 11.4 hours nonstop to Tehran.

The communications system is designed to provide direct links to palaces, the armed forces and civilian authorities.

The executive ship designed for His Imperial Majesty provides a great deal more than transportation.

It is a mobile headquarters for a nation, equipped so His Imperial Majesty retains the ability at all times to exercise his responsibilities as the National Executive Authority.

The communications package is based on the concept that His Imperial Majesty wants the same instant access to information he has while in residence.

Two other requirements: He must also enjoy the same direct communications ability to issue instructions to individuals in many locations; and transmissions must provide for privacy.

The executive airplane has instant access to existing systems.

The communications system provides all of these connections: Direct contact with international networks through linkages with landlines and communications satellites; VHF, UHF, and HF contact with armed forces, military headquarters, the integrated national command system, naval stations and ships at sea, civilian authorities, intelligence units and the intelligence center. A special system connects directly with the palace. Scramblers are included on both voice and teletype systems.

An interior arrangement designed for efficient work and comfortable relaxation.

The executive airplane is designed to make travel hours useful, productive and relaxing. Boeing engineers and designers have developed this unique cabin layout for His Imperial Majesty, drawing on their extensive experience in executive aircraft design, and with a sensitivity to the special requirements of a chief of state. To closely tailor the airplane to specific needs, many options are available within the basic configuration. In any arrangement there can be ample space for privacy for His Imperial Majesty, for the Royal Family, for conference work, for conducting normal business – plus comfortable, jetliner-style seating for staff and guests.

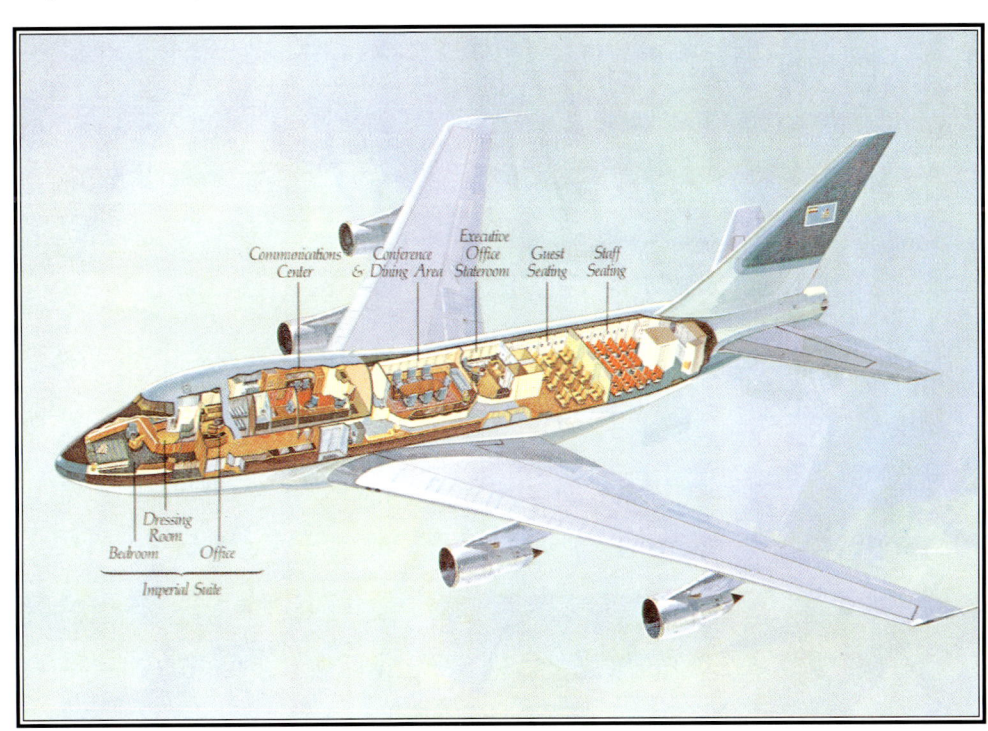

The Imperial Suite

The suite includes a bedroom, dressing room, and an office/reception area.

His Imperial Majesty's quarters are in the forward compartment of the ship for maximum quiet and privacy.

Access is tightly controlled: There is no traffic flow around the suite, and there is ample room for rest, study and relaxation in an area deliberately isolated from staff quarters and conference rooms.

The design is intended to help insure that His Imperial Majesty has both the comfort and the rest needed to remain refreshed in the course of conducting international business, even when long distances must be traveled.

37

Fixtures and appointments for the dressing room are designed to approximate the standards to which His Imperial Majesty and the Royal Family are accustomed.

The intent is to produce a travel environment with the least possible disruption of normal living patterns, permitting full concentration on the mission to be accomplished.

Quarters are roomy, comfortable, with many options in colors, textures and materials.

The office and reception area of the Imperial Suite is designed specifically for business. A private work area is built into the forward section of the office, with a comfortable seating area included to permit brief, casual conferences with staff members.

An adjacent area is designed for conferences on a more informal level and for staff work related to His Imperial Majesty's own activities in the office area.

The upper deck provides a secure area for the communications center.

The nerve center of the airplane is the upper deck – the cockpit and communications center. The location isolates the operators and equipment. Access stairs are designed to provide control of traffic to and from the center, and to give His Imperial Majesty access to the command areas without moving through other areas of the ship.

Conference and Dining

A spacious conference room – approximately 18 by 25 feet – is next to the office/reception area of the Imperial Suite. This arrangement permits conversion of the space from work room to dining area so that it may be used as a formal entertainment area should His Imperial Majesty wish to host guests while visiting a foreign country.

At His Imperial Majesty's command, military and civilian information received in the communications center can be channeled directly to his own office or the conference room.

When used for conferences, the audio-visual equipment permits slide, film, and videotape displays. Live on-board video is an attractive growth option.

Executive Office Stateroom

The executive ship includes office space for staff executives – a private, secure area where sensitive staff work can be conducted.

This area also can be a stateroom for use by His Imperial Majesty's special guests.

Guest and Staff Seating

The aft section of the main deck is divided into two cabins with airline-style seating for the comfort of staff and guests. Many configurations are possible, with various combinations of seating arrangements available to meet different mission requirements. The aft section includes galley and lavatory facilities adequate for up to 56 passengers.

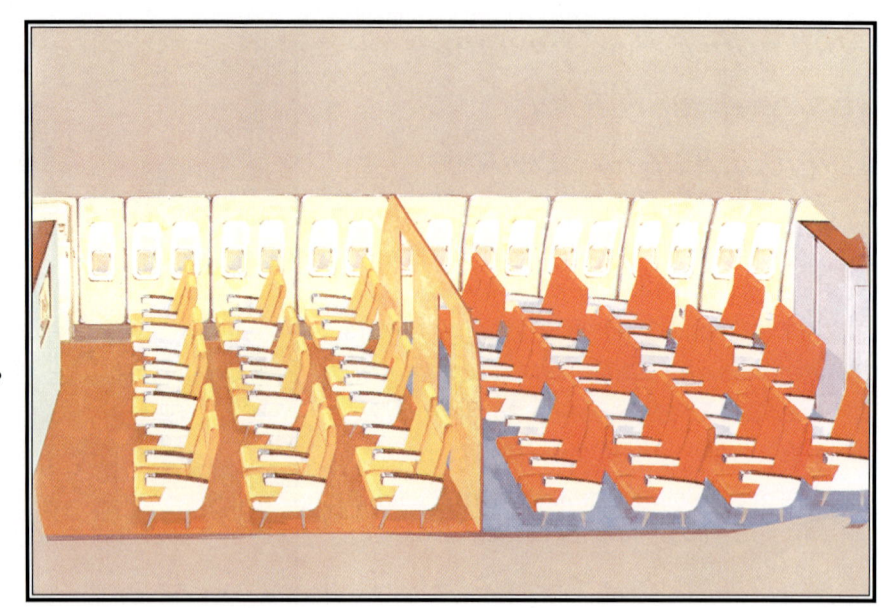

Cargo Capabilities

The holds provide abundant room for luggage, gifts, food, medical supplies or other cargo. Each hold can accommodate a car the size of a Mercedes 450 SEL so His Imperial Majesty and staff have the comfort, convenience, flexibility and security of personal ground transportation at all destinations.

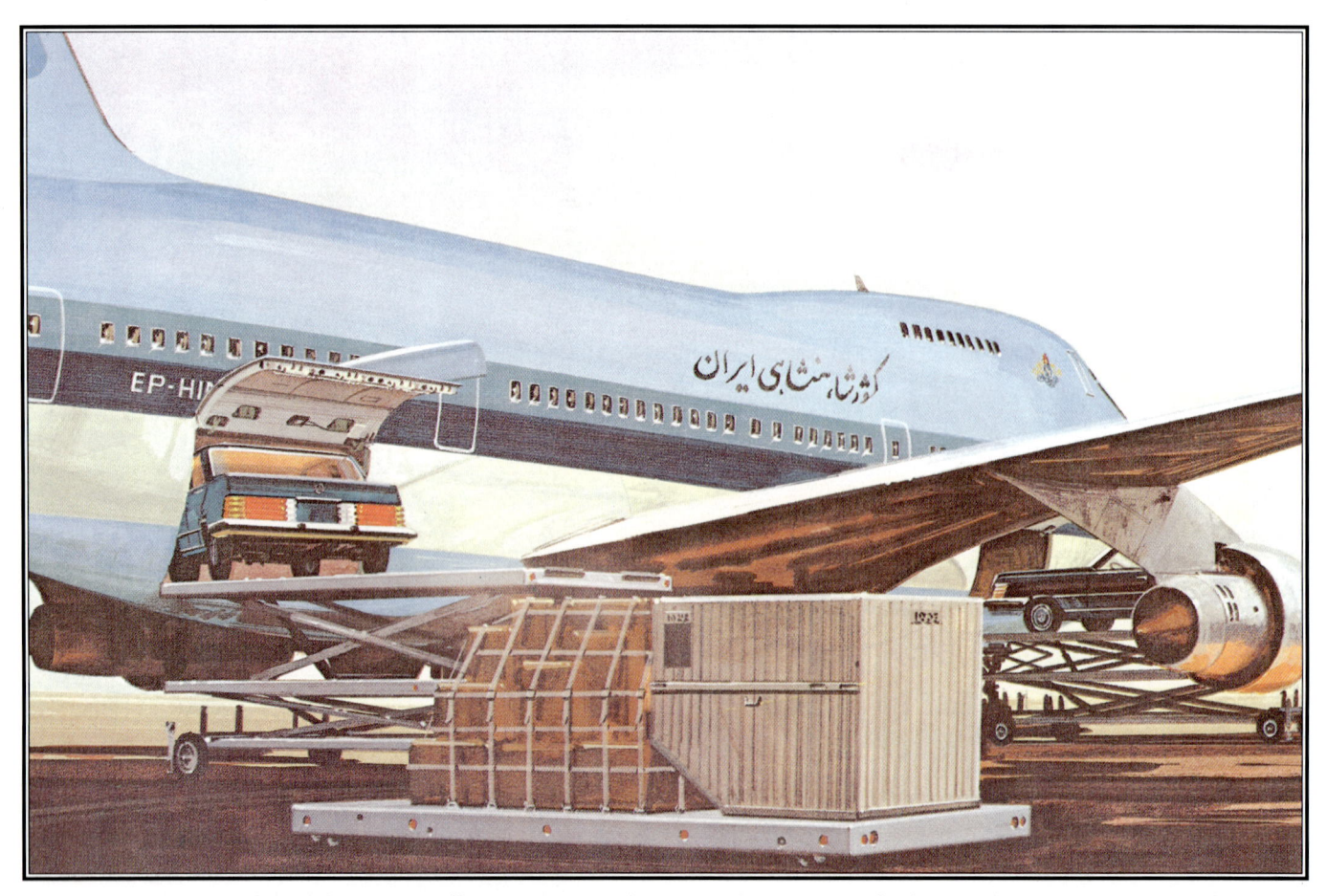

As an executive airplane, the 747SP offers His Imperial Majesty the support of advanced transportation and communications technology in dealing with important matters that influence both the domestic fortunes of Iran and the course of world affairs.

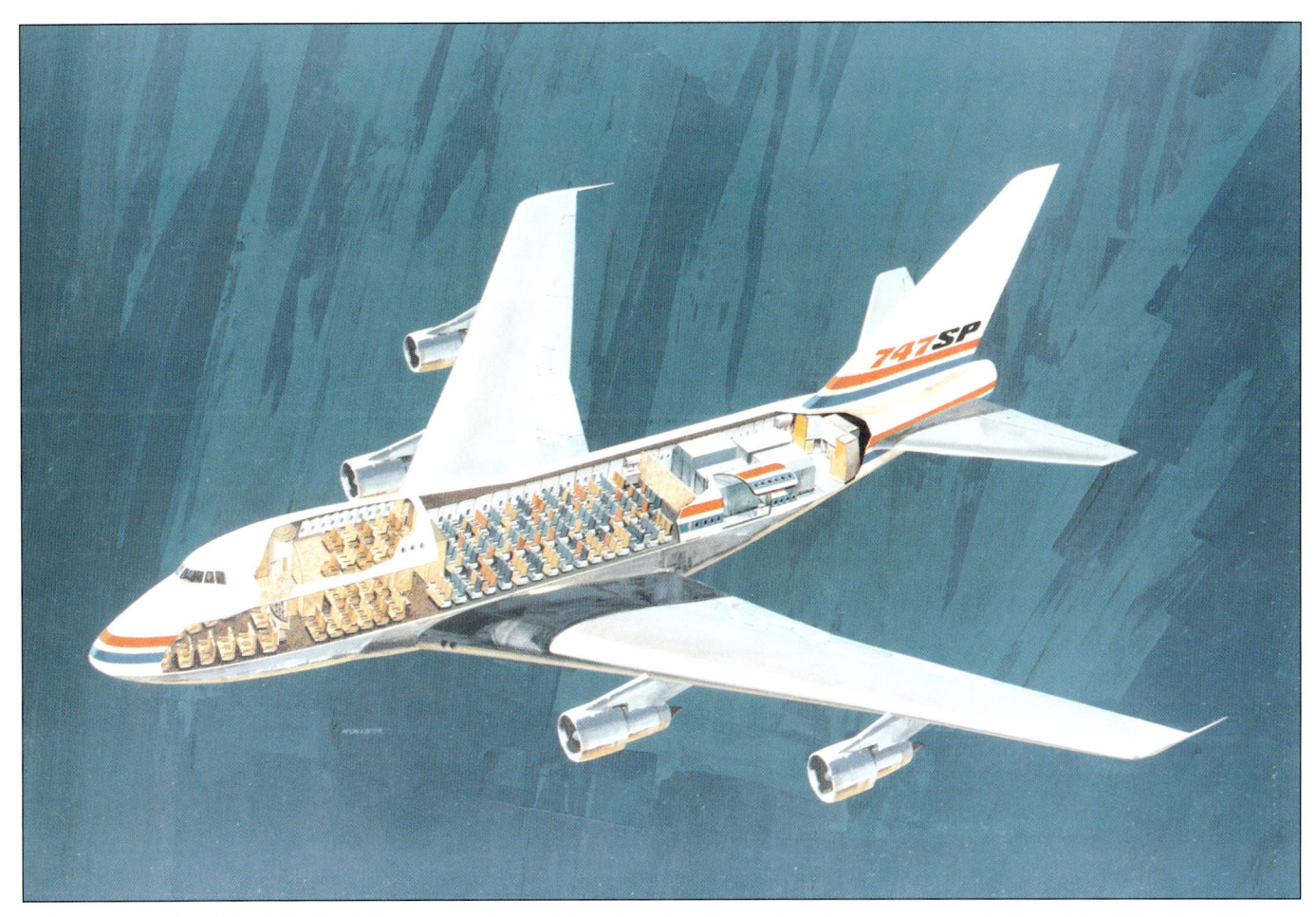

Cutaway view of the SP Combi in the 242-passenger/four-pallet configuration. The cargo section could be enlarged to carry eight cargo pallets, reducing passenger capacity to 186. Cargo could still be carried in the lower holds as well. (The Boeing Company Archives)

THE 747SP COMBI

Billed as "a new airplane with the flexibility to build passenger/cargo market share on growing international routes," the SP Combi was designed to be an efficient, profitable, all-in-one aircraft. With the installation of a large cargo door in the rear fuselage, the Combi could match the needs of an airline's current market by having the ability to easily shift from all passengers to a mix of passenger/cargo layouts. The SP Combi's 328-seat, all-passenger configuration could be quickly adjusted to carry either a 242-passenger/four-cargo pallet load or a 186-passenger/eight-pallet combination. The main deck pallets each measured 8 feet by 8 feet by 10 feet, and could be loaded side-by-side. The lower cargo holds would remain unchanged.

Boeing tried to sell the SP Combi as the perfect replacement for aging 707 and DC-8 narrow-body aircraft. A Combi sales brochure boasted that the SP could fly 186 passengers and 64,500 pounds of cargo farther, with better economics, than a 707-320C airliner with a full complement of 147 passengers and 6,800 pounds of cargo, and a 707-320C freighter filled with 58,000 pounds of cargo. Despite the excellent performance and economic projections and the popularity of the Combi option in the full size 747, the SP Combi found little interest with the airlines and none were produced.

A China Airlines SP (ln 304/msn 21300) was used to test the accessibility of the Combi's large, main deck cargo door with standard loading equipment. The "door" is outlined on the fuselage with removable black tape. The aircraft carries Boeing test registration N8290V but entered service as B-1862. (The Boeing Company Archives)

41

Chapter VI
THE RECORD SETTER

The 747SP set several speed and distance records even before entering commercial service. The aircraft showed what "Special Performance" truly meant on three spectacular flights around the world. Pan Am's *Clipper Liberty Bell* (N247SP, ln 268/msn 21023), shown here on a Boeing test flight, exudes a feeling of speed and grace in this photograph. (Museum of Flight Archives)

The reputation of the Boeing 747SP as the wide-body record setter was forever established by several dramatic delivery and demonstration flights around the world made by Pan American, South African Airways and United Airlines aircraft. The true nature of "Special Performance" was made evident on these passenger-carrying flights as the SP shattered numerous, long-standing speed and nonstop distance records while establishing new ones.

Three unofficial nonstop distance and speed records were set only four months after the first flight of the SP during Boeing's 29-day, worldwide demonstration tour in November and December 1975. N40135 (ln 273/msn 21025) flew 72,152 miles and accumulated 140 hours, 15 minutes of flight time. This aircraft made the first nonstop commercial jet flight from New York to Tokyo (7,030 miles in 13 hours, 33 minutes), the first nonstop wide-body airliner flight from Sydney to Santiago (7,143 miles in 12 hours, 14 minutes), and the first nonstop commercial flight from Mexico City to Belgrade (7,205 miles in 12 hours, 56 minutes).

South African Airways

A remarkable delivery flight took place on March 23-24, 1976, when South African Airways' first SP (ZS-SPA, ln 280/msn 21132) established a new world's distance record for commercial airplanes. The aircraft flew the 10,290-mile route from Boeing's Paine Field at Everett, Washington, to Cape Town nonstop. Departing Everett at 9:28 a.m. local time, the SP was airborne for a total of 17 hours, 22 minutes, arriving at Cape Town at 12:50 p.m. local time. Tailwinds over Bermuda registered as high as 129 miles per hour, which assisted in shaving several minutes off of the flight that was originally estimated to last 18 hours.

The SP reached it destination with 38,500 pounds of fuel remaining, which would have allowed an additional 2 hours, 27 minutes of flying time. The total weight of the record setting aircraft was 713,300 pounds, some 50,000 pounds more than the aircraft weighs in commercial service. The extra weight was due to the additional load of fuel contained in rubber-nylon bladders secured in the lower deck cargo holds. Aboard the flight were 26 South African government and airline officials, including S.L. Muller, Minister of Transport and Communications. Several important Boeing personnel also made the trip led by T.A. Wilson, Boeing Chairman. The SAA delivery flight broke the record for the longest flight by a commercial aircraft by 1,498 miles. The previous commercial aircraft distance record was set on February 23, 1962, by a Douglas DC-8-53, *Pacific Pacer* (N9608Z, ln 155/msn 45608) during an 8,792-mile flight from Tokyo to Miami.

In May of that same year, South African Airlines flew an SP between New York and Johannesburg without the usual refueling stop. The 224 passengers flew 8,010 miles in 13 hours, 42 minutes.

Auxiliary fuel tanks provided even greater range for the 10,290-mile delivery flight of the first South African Airways SP. The aircraft set the world's distance record for commercial aircraft on its historic nonstop flight from Everett, Washington, to Cape Town. After completing the flight, the SP still had two hours and 27 minutes of fuel remaining onboard. (The Boeing Company Archives)

Clipper Liberty Bell

Pan American provided a dramatic example of what could be done with the brand new Boeing on a two-stop flight around the world. N533PA (ln 273/msn 21025), the same aircraft that introduced the SP to the far corners of the globe during the 1975 demonstration tour (then as N40135), was called upon again. The aircraft had been christened *Clipper Liberty Bell* in honor of the upcoming American bicentennial celebration (Pan Am switched names with N531PA, which was now called *Clipper Freedom*). The goal of the flight was to beat the existing around-the-world record for a commercial aircraft of 62 hours, 27 minutes, 35 seconds, set by a Flying Tiger Line Boeing 707-349C named *Pole Cat* (N322F, ln 445/msn 18975) flying over both poles from November 15-17, 1965. A second around-the-world record of 45 hours, 19 minutes – set by three B-52 bombers nearly 20 years earlier – was also within reach.

A total of 98 revenue passengers signed up for Clipper 200 – "Liberty Bell Express" – paying $2,912 for a first-class seat and $1,838 for a coach-class ticket. Led by Captain Walter Mulliken, Pan Am Vice President and Chief Pilot, the carefully planned flight departed from John F. Kennedy International Airport in New York on May 1, 1976. The journey began with the nonstop trip to New Delhi – an 8,081-mile flight that took 13 hours, 31 minutes. Total amount of fuel consumed on this segment of the trip totaled 41,099 gallons, yet enough remained for the SP to continue on to Bangkok, Thailand with sufficient reserves. After a 2-hour stop, the flight continued to Japan. Head winds slowed the 7,539-mile flight to an elapsed time of 14 hours, 1 minute. A 2-hour break was scheduled at Haneda International Airport, but a non-mechanical problem caused a significant holdup. Ground workers at the airport were in the midst of a labor dispute and used the Pan Am flight to bring attention to their demands. Just as the flight was ready to depart, several ground service vehicles were parked behind the SP, causing a two-hour delay. While negotiations with the strikers were under way, an additional 12,000 pounds of fuel was added to allow for faster than planned speeds, in an attempt to make up precious lost time on the final leg.

The delay in Tokyo ruled out the possibility of beating the B-52's elapsed time, but the commercial record was still well within reach. The last segment of 7,517 miles was made in a brisk 11 hours, 53 minutes. *Liberty Bell* arrived in New York on May 3, with a total takeoff-to-landing elapsed time of 46 hours, 50 seconds, covering 23,137 miles. The flight times, verified by the National Aeronautics Association, beat the 707's record by 16 hours, 24 minutes. Actual flying time around the world was 39 hours, 25 minutes, 53 seconds.

Clipper New Horizons

On August 2, 1977, the Associated Press reported that Pan American World Airways had asked the Civil Aeronautics Board for permission to fly a Boeing 747 on an around-the-world flight over the North and South Poles, to celebrate the carrier's 50th anniversary. "Tickets on the flight, which will attempt to set a record, will sell to the public at $3,333 a person first class and $2,222 for coach. There will be movies, a fashion show, a strolling musician, and a hairdresser. There will be four separate flight crews." With that announcement, the general public was again allowed the rare opportunity to participate in aviation history, on the first passenger flight around-the-world over both poles.

Flight 50 departed San Francisco on October 28, 1977 – 50 years to the day after Pan American started service from Key West, Florida, to Havana, Cuba. It would fly a route over the North Pole to London; to Cape Town, South Africa; over the South Pole; to Auckland, New Zealand; and return to San Francisco on October 30. One hundred seventy-two passengers (including the author) felt the need for

Pan Am Flight 50 (N533PA, ln 273/msn 21025) on the ramp at San Francisco International Airport just prior to departure. The aircraft carried special "Flight 50" logos during the flight. (Author)

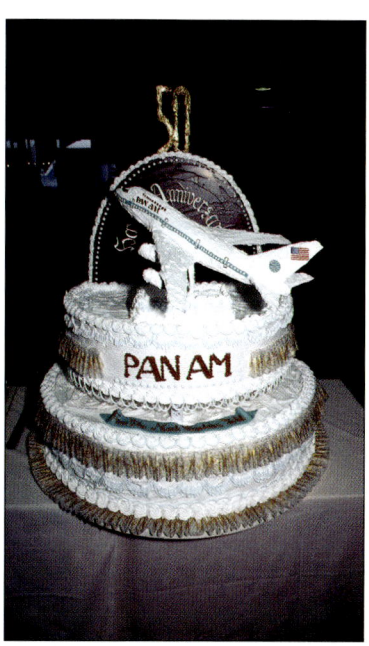

Pan American celebrated its 50th birthday in style with a 54-hour flight around the world over both poles. (Author)

adventure and purchased tickets for this once-in-a-lifetime experience, and the flight was sold out in three days. The 747SP used for this odyssey, N533PA (ln 273/msn 21025), earned the distinction of being the only aircraft in history to fly around the world via the equator (as *Clipper Liberty Bell*) and over the poles (as *Clipper New Horizons*). Again, the time to beat was the Flying Tigers' 62 hours, 27 minutes, 35 seconds time set flying over the poles.

A pre-flight birthday party was thrown in San Francisco for the passengers, who then boarded the flight and departed for a 6,403-mile trip to London. The manifest for the flight included Harry F. Byrd, grandson of Admiral Richard E. Byrd; Janelle Commissiong, Miss Universe; and Kimberly Tomes, Miss USA. As the SP neared the North Pole, Captain Walter H. Mulliken (pilot of the Clipper 200 flight) announced the arrival with a countdown. Champagne toasts were made as the aircraft circled the pole and then put on a course for London. A Gucci fashion show took place aboard, featuring the beauty

Here's to the top of the world! Flight attendants celebrate the passing of the first major milestone – flying directly over the North Pole – with a champagne toast. (Author)

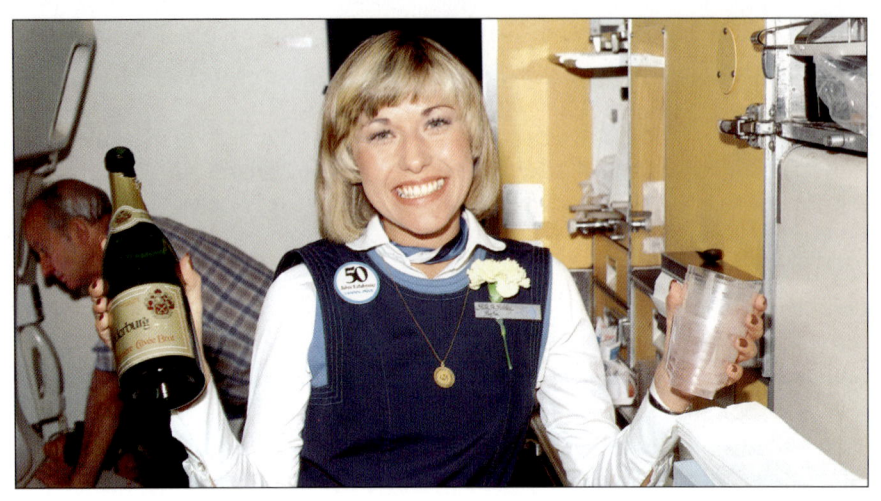

On the way to New Zealand, Rita Pickley-Adragna dispenses fine South African wines and plenty of good cheer. (Author)

Walter Mulliken, veteran circumnavigator. Captain Mulliken commanded Pan Am's record-setting, around-the-world flights of *Clipper Liberty Bell* and *Clipper New Horizons*. (Author)

The desolate beauty of Antarctica from 41,000 feet. (Author)

Clipper New Horizons rests for a brief two hours on the rain-washed tarmac at Auckland. N533PA is the only aircraft to have circled the world at the equator and over the poles. (Author)

The three-inch bronze medallion issued to all passengers aboard Pan Am Flight 50 by Pratt and Whitney. The reverse side featured the engine maker's famous emblem. (Author)

queens, Gucci models and even a member of the cabin crew. Flight 50 was welcomed at Heathrow by John Beasley, Mayor of the Borough of Hillingdon. A brief 2-hour stop for fuel, a ceremony and the addition of Miss England, and then the flight was on its way to South Africa.

Other than crossing the equator for the first time, the 6,157-mile leg between London and Cape Town was uneventful, and many passengers slept in anticipation of things to come. A lovely evening reception with cheese, fruit and a seemingly unlimited supply of fine South African wines awaited the travelers during their short stay in Cape Town. Disappointment in not being able to see that beautiful city quickly passed as Flight 50 crossed the huge expanses of Antarctica on its 7,523-mile journey to Auckland.

As the SP approached the South Pole, the passengers were treated to more of the fine food Pan Am had prepared. One of the menu items boarded in South Africa was "Saddle of Springbok." As Flight 50 was chased across the ice and snow by the shadow of the contrail, passengers and crew alike were overwhelmed by the vastness of Antarctica. The pilots were in contact with the scientists below at McMurdo Sound (their C-130 was on call in case of any emergency with the Pan Am flight). The only request from those lonely guys on the ground was to hear the sound of a woman's voice, and in the spirit, a stewardess and Miss USA were happy to oblige. Over much too quickly, the SP left Antarctica and the South Pole behind for a 3 a.m. arrival in New Zealand. More tables filled with food were waiting when the SP arrived in rain-soaked Auckland. Maori dancers had Miss South Africa (who joined up in Cape Town), Miss New Zealand, and even Captain Mulliken and his crew join them for some traditional dances. Exhilarated but becoming exhausted, the passengers boarded their trusty SP for the last (and longest) leg of the trip to San Francisco.

The sunrise was warm and bright over the little islands of the South Pacific. Most passengers were dozing as the plane sped 6,608 miles on its way into the history books. Wheels down brought a huge cheer from everyone aboard and more cheers when Captain Mulliken asked the passengers over the PA system if they would do it again. When the tires touched down in San Francisco, the digital timer aboard was stopped at 54 hours, 7 minutes, 12 seconds – a world's record for speed around the world over the Earth's poles. Pan American Flight 50 flew 26,230 miles and set six additional world's records which were certified by the Fédération Aéronautique Internationale (FAI):

- Speed between the Earth's poles: 27 hours, 20 minutes, 45 seconds; 458.68 mph.
- Speed between two points of the equator over a pole: 27 hours, 47 minutes, 40 seconds; 474.03 mph.
- Speed over a recognized course, San Francisco-London via the North Pole; 11 hours, 14 minutes, 36 seconds; 558.51 mph.
- Speed over a commercial air route, London-Cape Town: 11 hours, 6 minutes; 542.51 mph.
- Speed over a recognized course, Cape Town-Auckland: 14 hours, 8 minutes, 9 seconds; 534.43 mph.
- Speed over a commercial air route, Auckland-San Francisco; 11 hours, 34 minutes; 565.52 mph.

Actual flying time was 48 hours, 3 minutes.

Friendship One

Although Pan Am was to survive into the 1990s, no more record-setting flights were planned. When United bought the Pacific routes from Pan Am, the SPs went with them. When the opportunity came up for the SP to set a world's record, United jumped at the chance by "loaning" the airplane to pilot Clay Lacy and his crews. Of course, the goal of this flight was to set a new record for flying around the world, but there was more to the flight than just setting a record. *Friendship One*, as the flight would be known, would raise money for the children's charities sponsored by the Friendship Foundation. Passengers could book a seat by paying a minimum donation of $5,000. The 141-person manifest included such notable names as Apollo 11 astronaut Neal Armstrong; former test pilots Bob Hoover and Gen. Laurence Craigie and Moya Lear, widow of Lear Jet founder, Bill Lear.

In addition to United providing the aircraft, The Boeing Company, Pratt and Whitney and Volkswagen of America donated fuel and other required flight services.

The time to beat for this flight was 45 hours, 25 minutes, 55 seconds, set by a Gulfstream III business jet. Captain Lacy said "Our goal is to shave at least six hours off the old record." The Museum of Flight at Boeing Field in Seattle established an elaborate ground base communication center called Mission Control to provide hourly updates and track the progress of *Friendship One* en route. The 23,125-mile route was selected based on historic wind patterns; the stops (Athens and Taipei) were chosen because of their strategic locations, refueling facilities and good weather. After departing the Museum of Flight, the SP flew nonstop to Athens. 46,000 pounds of fuel were taken on board, drinking water was replenished, the lavatories were serviced and the oil was checked. Olympic Airways, which provided all ground services free of charge, had mechanics standing by. The same process was repeated at Taipei. The time spent on the ground was limited to 45 minutes or less, and the passengers did not deplane.

The flight was a complete success, establishing a new absolute speed record of 36 hours, 54 minutes, 15 seconds. Best of all the Friendship Foundation netted over $500,000 for children's charities. Capt. Lacy said in a post-flight interview that he was confident that the record would stand for years. It lasted less than a month, beaten by a Gulfstream IV business jet, which made the trip in 36 hours, 8 minutes.

Diplôme de Record from *Friendship One* Certificate awarded by the Fédération Aéronautique Internationale to pilot Clay Lacy and co-pilot Vern Jobst for their command of *Friendship One*. United loaned the SP to the Friendship Foundation as the means for raising over a half-million dollars for children's charities around the world. (Museum of Flight Archives)

Friendship One (N147UA, ln 331/msn 21548) is tugged into place onto the ramp at the Museum of Flight on Boeing Field in Seattle prior to departure. The aircraft would return to the museum to complete its 36-hour, 54-minute, 15-second flight around the world. (Jay P. Spenser)

Chapter VII
INITIAL OPERATORS

One-ninth of the entire 747SP production is shown on the Everett Division ramp at Paine Field in April 1980. The five aircraft are seen in various stages of completion. At the top, China Airlines B-1880 (ln 445/msn 22298) prepares to depart to the runway for taxi tests. Braniff International Airways N604BN (ln 413/msn 21786) has just returned from a test flight (center), while a second Braniff SP N606BN (ln 447/21992) awaits installation of its four Pratt and Whitney JT9D-7 engines (lower center). The first two TWA SPs, N58201 (ln 415/msn 21961, top left) and N57202 (ln 439/msn 21962, center right) await delivery.

Other aircraft on the ramp include a Cathay Pacific 747-267B (VR-HIA, ln 446/msn 21966), British Airways 747-236B (G-BDXJ, ln 440/msn 21831) and a full-size 747-227B painted in Braniff colors (N605BN, ln 437/msn 21991). This aircraft was not taken up by the struggling Texas-based airline but would eventually be delivered to Northwest Orient as N633US. A 747-212B (9V-SQN, ln 449/msn 21939) for Singapore Airlines, fresh from the paint hangar, awaits engines. Also of interest, at the top right corner, an unidentified 747-2L5B Combi aircraft, one of two originally built for Libyan Arab Airlines, is parked awaiting a new owner. (Museum of Flight Archives)

Pan Am *Clipper Liberty Bell* N531PA (ln 268/msn 21023) is readied for delivery. The Boeing test registration, N247SP, has been replaced with Pan Am's civil registration, and the test equipment is in the process of being removed. (The Boeing Company Archives)

The argument of whether or not the Boeing 747SP program was a success is still open to interpretation. The fact is, in a 13-year period from March 5, 1976, to December 9, 1989, only 45 SPs were delivered to 14 customers – an average of 3.5 aircraft per year. As a stand-alone program, these numbers would have been disastrous for any manufacturer. However, the overall lack of sales does not seem quite so bleak when viewed from the perspective of Boeing management. The SP served its purpose by keeping valuable customers who certainly would have obtained wide-body aircraft from the competition, and it satisfied operators who continue to purchase large numbers of Boeing wide-body jets. Nine of the 14 customers ordering the SP from Boeing were prior 747 operators (Braniff, China Airlines, Iraqi Airways, Korean, Pan Am, Saudia, South African, Qantas and TWA). The remaining five initial operators were first-time 747 buyers (CAAC, Government of Abu Dhabi, Government of Saudi Arabia, Iran Air and Syrianair). Of the latter group, CAAC and the Government of Saudi Arabia purchased more of the full-size Boeing jumbos (it could also be supposed, politics aside, that Iran Air and Syrianair would have continued to supplement their Boeing fleets). Of the 40 surviving SP aircraft, 27 – or 68 percent – are still either owned or operated on lease-back by the initial operator or a subsidiary company. This speaks well for the reliability and long-term usefulness of the aircraft. The following is a summary of each of the airlines purchasing the 747SP, arranged by order date. A complete service history for each aircraft can be found in Appendix I, Individual Aircraft Disposition.

Pan American World Airways

Starting with an order for six of the then-gigantic Boeing 314 flying boats in 1936, Pan American became the launch customer for several significant new types of long-range Boeing aircraft. It introduced the first pressurized airliner, the 307 Stratoliner, the double-deck 377 Stratocruiser; the 707, America's first jetliner; and the largest airliner ever built, the 747. Once again, Pan Am led the way with the Special Performance 747. An almost perfect design for Pan Am's requirements, the SP gave the airline the ability to streamline its wide-body fleet, permitted a greater degree of year-round wide-body service, and allowed for earlier introduction of wide-body jets in markets where the capacity of the full-size 747 was not required.

An announcement was made jointly by Boeing and Pan American on September 10, 1973, for 25 SPs (10 firm orders and options for 15 more), subject to satisfactory financing arrangements. Delivery of the new jets was scheduled to begin in early 1976, with the options slotted for arrival between 1977 and

1979. The total purchase price for the firm orders was $28 million each, including spares and "related ground equipment." On April 15, 1974, as a reflection of the airline's mounting financial troubles, a revised contract was signed between Pan Am and Boeing. The total number remained the same as in the original agreement, but were modified to seven firm orders and 18 options.

Yet another change in the contract was to come on August 1, 1974, when Pan Am announced plans to lease five SPs under terms of an agreement worked out between The Boeing Company, Northrop Corp., United Aircraft Corp. and Citicorp Leasing. The leases would be for a two-year period; the first was scheduled for February 1976. Again, the total numbers did not change as Pan Am retained options for 20 additional aircraft. William Seawell, Pan Am Board Chairman and Chief Executive Officer, said the "current economic situation has precluded a more conventional acquisition of the SP in favor of the short-term lease agreement." Seawell also noted "Our enthusiasm for the SP is undiminished. Acquisition of the aircraft at this time is an integral part of a long-range recovery plan for the airline."

As a reflection of the spirit which surrounded the upcoming bicentennial celebration, the five new SP "Clippers" were given names which reflect American pride: *Mayflower, Liberty Bell, Constitution, Freedom* and *Great Republic*.

Pan American's first SP, *Clipper Freedom* (N533PA, ln 273/msn 21025), was delivered on March 5, 1976. The aircraft, a veteran of Boeing's 72,152-mile worldwide demonstration tour, was ferried from the 747 plant at Everett, Washington, to Seattle-Tacoma International Airport immediately after delivery. The new SP was the 2,800th commercial jetliner delivered by Boeing since the first 707-121 (N709PA, ln 3/msn 17588) was accepted by Pan Am on August 15, 1958. In order to make the most of its first flight for the airline, N533PA was loaded with cargo destined for New York.

Other deliveries quickly followed: *Clipper Constitution* (N532PA, ln 270/msn 21024) on March 29, 1976, *Clipper Mayflower* (N530PA, ln 265/msn 21022) on April 26, *Clipper Liberty Bell* (N531PA, ln 268/msn 21023) on May 12, and *Clipper Great Republic* (N534PA, ln 286/msn 21026) on May 28. The SP offered Pan Am the ability to open new nonstop routes around the world. Scheduled SP service began on April 25, 1976, when the airline began daily service from Los Angeles to Tokyo.

One day later, Pan Am made good use of the SP's range by inaugurating the first nonstop service between New York and Tokyo – a 13.5-hour voyage which shaved about 3.5 hours off flight times requiring a refueling stop. Flight 801 operated westbound on Mondays, Thursdays and Saturdays. The eastbound service (PA 800) departed Tokyo on Wednesdays, Fridays and Sundays. The nonstop flights became so popular that the frequency was expanded to daily service the following August. By July 1976, less than three months after the start of service, schedule reliability for the new aircraft was 96 percent – even higher than the standard 747 fleet average. Load factors remained high, and Pan Am was utilizing the aircraft 10.9 block hours per day on average, with plans to increase to 13.8 hours in August 1976. Routes for the new aircraft were expanded to Europe, Bahrain and South America.

Pan American pulled out all the stops to celebrate the arrival of its new 747SP and the 1976 American bicentennial celebration. N533PA was utilized for a special mission, to fly a 23,132-mile route from New York to New Delhi, Tokyo, and back to New York in the record-setting time of 46 hours, 50 seconds. In honor of this event, Pan Am changed the aircraft name from *Clipper Freedom* to *Clipper Liberty Bell* (and N531PA, the former *Clipper Liberty Bell*, became *Clipper Freedom*).

On December 8, 1976, Pan Am SPs began the fastest service by any airline between the United States and the South Pacific. Flight 815 left San Francisco on Wednesdays and Fridays, flying nonstop to Auckland, New Zealand. The flight arrived Fridays and Sundays after crossing the International Date Line, continuing with a short leg to Melbourne, Australia. The Wednesday flight originated in New York, providing the only direct, single-plane service from the U.S. East Coast to the South Pacific. Return flight 816 left Sydney on Sundays, flying nonstop (a 7,475-mile, 13-hour, 15-minute flight) to San Francisco, and continuing on to New York. Flight 816 had the distinction of being the longest scheduled nonstop route in the world.

On Wednesdays, 816 flew from Sydney to Auckland, then 6,750 miles nonstop to San Francisco. The fleet was expanded again on December 9, 1976, when the sixth Pan Am SP was ordered (N536PA, ln 306/msn 21441). Upon delivery to Pan Am in May 1977, the aircraft was christened *Clipper Lindbergh* by Anne Morrow Lindbergh, widow of aviator Charles Lindbergh, to commemorate the 50th anniversary of his solo trans-Atlantic flight. SPs number seven (*Clipper High Flyer*, N537PA, ln 325/msn 21547) and eight (*Clipper Fleetwing*, N538PA, ln 331/msn 21548) were ordered on July 9, 1977.

The SP was once again given an opportunity to show its Special Performance stuff on a flight around the world – this time to celebrate Pan American's 50th anniversary. Only Pan Am would be able to pull off a trip with such a unique routing – the first passenger flight flown over both the North and South Poles. Departing from San Francisco on October 28, 1977, N533PA would make the flight over the North Pole to London, Cape Town, over the South Pole to Auckland, and back to San Francisco in 54 hours, 7 minutes, 12 seconds. In the process of making this flight, the SP set seven world speed and distance records. Again, the name of N533PA was changed for a round-the-world flight, this time from *Clipper Liberty Bell* to *Clipper New Horizons*. In addition to flying Boeing's worldwide demonstration tour (then as N40135), N533PA holds the distinction of being the only aircraft to fly around the world both at the equator and over the poles.

On December 15, 1977, orders were placed for two more SPs, bringing the total to 10. *Clipper Black Hawk* (N539PA, ln 367/msn 21648) and *Clipper White Falcon* (N540PA, ln 373/msn 21649) were scheduled for delivery in the Spring of 1979. The final SP received by Pan Am, *Clipper America* (N529PA, ln 447/msn 21992) would be purchased second-hand from the now-defunct Braniff International Airways on September 23, 1983.

On February 1, 1979, Pan Am introduced "sleeperette" seats on five routes, expanding to six (Los Angeles–London) by that summer. The seats offered a 63-inch pitch, and reclined to 60 degrees for sleeping. Sleeperettes were available between New York–Tokyo, Los Angeles–Tokyo, Los Angeles–Auckland, New York–Dhahran, and New York–Buenos Aires for first-class passengers at no extra charge. At mealtime, passengers traveling together could have their first-class seat trays linked to provide a single "banquette" table. The SPs were configured to carry 42 of the sleeper seats.

On April 22, 1985, in an attempt to stem the drain of negative cash flow, Pan Am sold off its Pacific routes (almost a quarter of its network, and perhaps its most valuable remaining asset) to United Airlines for $750 million. The sale included all 11 of the 747SPs. On February 11, 1986, The SP fleet was received by United, and the aircraft were re-registered. Unfortunately, selling the Pacific routes was not enough to stop Pan Am's free fall, and on December 4, 1991, the "World's Most Experienced Airline," ceased to exist.

The 11 aircraft owned by Pan American and United have gone to numerous owners and operators. Unfortunately, the first five aircraft have been dismantled for spares. One (ln 306/msn 21441) will fly into the next century as the Stratospheric Observatory for Infrared Astronomy (SOFIA). Two more are stored in Marana, Arizona, awaiting new owners. The former N539PA currently flies for the government of Qatar as VP-BAT, while N540PA operates as VIP transportation for the government of Brunei. N529PA (formerly N606BN) has been converted for use by the Sultan of Oman.

Over the years several changes were made to the Pan American livery. All of its SPs were delivered with the familiar black titles, powder blue cheatline and globe on the tail. The first minor change was to stop the cheatline at the edge of the radome with a diagonal "cut." This new look made it easier to swap damaged radomes without having mismatched paint stripes. A thicker cheatline followed, and finally the Pan Am "billboard" titles appeared. This last livery retained the same white fuselage, but replaced the cheatline and small black titles with six-feet-high blue letters. The aircraft names appeared in blue lettering on the forward fuselage, about halfway between the cockpit and window line.

Iran Air

The second airline to order and operate the 747SP was Iran Air. A firm order for two SPs, plus options for two more, were placed on October 10, 1973, with the aircraft scheduled for delivery in March and May 1976. A third firm order was placed on June 18, 1974, to arrive in May 1977. Iran Air was the first foreign SP customer, bolstering Boeing's confidence in its decision to proceed.

The airline's first SP (EP-IAA, ln 275/msn 20998) was delivered on March 12, 1976, but remained at Boeing Field through the end of that month for flight crew training. Two flight training courses for 16 pilots and eight flight engineers were completed at the Boeing Flight Center in Seattle. Delivery of the new SP enabled Iran Air to begin nonstop (eastbound) service in June 1976, on the 6,296-mile New York-to-Tehran route.

Because of Tehran's 3,949-foot altitude and headwinds, the westbound flight made an intermediate stop at London-Heathrow. Load factors on this route were reported to be 90 percent and higher.

The second SP (EP-IAB, ln 278/msn 20999) was delivered on May 10, 1976, and the third (EP-IAC, ln 307/msn 21093) on May 27, 1977. A fourth and final SP was ordered in June 1, 1978, but political developments created problems for handing over the aircraft.

Because of the overthrow of the Shah and the coming to power of the Islamic fundamentalist government, EP-IAD (ln 371/msn 21758) was received in an unusual manner. Painted all-white with a bare aluminum hull, it was ferried from Everett to Frankfurt, Germany, then unceremoniously delivered on July 12, 1979.

The first 747SP destined for Iran Air (EP-IAA, ln 275/msn 20998) on the Boeing flightline at Everett. Delivered on March 12, 1976, the aircraft would be used on the New York–Tehran route. (The Boeing Company Archives)

The basic livery has remained largely unchanged since delivery. EP-IAA, -IAB and -IAC still have the original blue cheatline and an ancient symbol of Persia – the mythical Homa Bird – on the tail. The original black titles were made smaller and the sub-title "The Airline of the Islamic Republic of Iran" was added. The flag was removed from the tail, enlarged and placed in front of the titles. EP-IAD has a more modern, all-white body and bolder fuselage titles, and a larger bird on the tail. The flag and inscription remain but are now placed behind the Iran Air titles. The first three aircraft are named after Iranian provinces. These titles are carried below the cheatline, in front of the pitot tubes. The names have been transferred between aircraft: EP-IAA, *Kurdistan* (previously *Fars*); EP-IAB, *Khorasan* (previously *Kurdistan*); and EP-IAC, *Fars* (previously *Khuzestan*).

Flight test on this aircraft (ln 371/msn 21758) was started prior to painting. All exposed portions of the new aluminum skin are covered by a green protective coating while the aircraft awaits its turn in the paint hangar. Due to the political situation in Iran, the SP initially carried Boeing registration number N1800B and was later delivered to Frankfurt, Germany, without titles except for registration EP-IAD. (The Boeing Company Archives)

South African Airways

The second-largest operator of the 747SP after Pan Am/United, South African Airways (SAA) received six of the aircraft. The SP's long range was exceptionally well-suited to SAA's route structure. Firm orders for three aircraft (ZS-SPA, ln 280/msn 21132, -SPB, ln 282/msn 21133, and -SPC, ln 288/msn 21134) were announced on July 16, 1974. The total value of the order was placed at about $87 million ($29 million each). Deliveries took place on March 23, April 23, and June 17, 1976. Two more aircraft (ZS-SPD, ln 293/msn 21253 and -SPE, ln 298/msn 21254) were ordered on August 28, 1975, with an option for a third SP. Two months later, SAA became the largest purchaser of the SP with its sixth order (ZS-SPF, ln 301/msn 21263).

The first SAA SP aircraft was placed in scheduled service on May 1, 1976, on a Johannesburg–Athens–Lisbon–Rome routing. After the second aircraft was delivered, a weekly Johannesburg–New York (via Sal Island) service began on August 1, 1976. This new flight saved at least 2.5 hours over the Johannesburg–Rio de Janeiro–New York routing.

On the delivery flight from Everett, Washington, to Cape Town, ZS-SPA flew a distance of 10,290 miles nonstop in 17 hours and 22 minutes. This flight took place on March 23-24, 1976, and set a

About to set a commercial aircraft distance record on its 10,290-mile nonstop delivery flight to Cape Town, South African Airways ZS-SPA *Matroosberg* (ln 280/msn 21132) receives final inspection before handover. (The Boeing Company Archives)

world's distance record for commercial airliners. Two months later, a SAA SP with 224 passengers aboard flew nonstop from New York to Johannesburg, a distance of 8,010 miles in 13 hours and 42 minutes.

In 1984, South African Airways began sub-leasing the SPs to other carriers. Air Malawi, Air Mauritius, Alliance, Avia, Cameroon Airlines, Luxair, Namib Air (later Air Namibia), Royal Air Maroc, Trek Airways and UTA have made use of the six SAA SPs. First to leave South African ownership was ZS-SPD; it was leased to Royal Air Maroc on March 15, 1985, and later purchased by the airline. ZS-SPB was acquired by Panair Inc., which leased it briefly to Cameroon Airlines. The four remaining aircraft are still in service. ZS-SPA is leased to Alliance; ZS-SPC and ZS-SPE are currently with SAA; ZS-SPF is leased to Air Namibia and registered as V5-SPF.

The South African livery has been slightly revised since the first delivery. The delivery colors featured a white upper fuselage, blue cheatline, and an orange trimline and tail. The tail sported a white and blue flash and the flying springbok insignia in black. The titles on the port side (South African Airways) were in English, the starboard side (Suid-Afrikaanse Lugdiens) in Afrikaans. A more modern look was later established by using large SAA/SAL titles in addition to the name in smaller letters. The flash was removed from the tail and the springbok was enlarged. The orange trimline was made wider. Several temporary variations to the SAA livery have been noted (i.e. odd color stripes on tail fin). This is usually due to a hasty cover-up after the aircraft returned from lease with another airline. On the early livery, the aircraft name appears on the forward fuselage under the cheatline. Names were moved above the cheatline with the newer colors.

Syrianair

Syrian Arab Airlines (Syrianair) was not a typical SP customer, since its primary use of the type was limited to medium-range, high-density routes. On December 6, 1974, in an effort to modernize an aging fleet, Syrianair spent over $100 million on two 747SP (YK-AHA, ln 284/msn 21174 and YK-AHB, ln 290/msn 21175) and three Advanced 727-200 jetliners. The SPs were delivered on May 21, and July 16, 1976, and placed into service on the Damascus–London route. Both operate regional flights from Damascus throughout Europe and the Middle East.

Syrianair has not made any changes to its colors since delivery of the aircraft from Boeing. The livery features a white bird on the blue tail fin, and a blue cheatline. A round insignia, the symbol of the political party of the Arab Union, appears on the forward fuselage. Aircraft names *November 16* (YK-AHA), and *Arab Solidarity* (YK-AHB) appear in English and Arabic in front of the first entry door.

Syrianair YK-AHA *November 16* (ln 284/msn 21174) is prepared for a pre-delivery test flight. One of the few airlines to retain original delivery livery, the Syrianair uses its SPs on international flights to and from Damascus. (The Boeing Company Archives)

China Airlines

The distinction of being the first airline in Asia to purchase the 747SP (and the fifth overall) went to China Airlines. The announcement of the agreement to purchase one 747SP was made by General Cliff Louie, China Airline Chairman and President, in Seattle on February 3, 1976. General Louie stated that the purchase was "the most significant and major equipment decision ever made by China Airlines." The aircraft (B-1862, ln 304/msn 21300) was delivered on April 6, 1977, and began nonstop service from Taipei to both San Francisco and Los Angeles on May 18. The interior featured tapestry designs from the Ming Dynasty, good luck symbols and a 15-seat (nine berthable), upper deck lounge.

Routes for the new SP included twice-weekly Hong Kong–Taipei–San Francisco service, and a once-weekly Hong Kong–Taipei–Los Angeles flight. On December 8, 1978, an agreement was announced for the purchase of a second SP. B-1880 (ln 445/msn 22298) would be delivered on April 30, 1980. The third China Airlines 747SP was ordered in March 1980 (N4508H, ln 534/msn 22547) and delivered on September 30, 1980. As its service continued to grow, China Airlines ordered a fourth SP. N4522V was

The first airline in Asia to purchase the 747SP, China Airlines considered the acquisition of its first SP to be "the most significant and major equipment decision ever made by China Airlines." N4508H (ln 534/msn 22547) was the third SP delivered to the carrier. (The Boeing Company Archives)

delivered on June 29, 1982 as the last passenger-configured 747SP built (the final two are VIP aircraft). All four aircraft served with China Airlines until they were leased to subsidiary, Mandarin Airlines, and painted in full Mandarin colors.

The China Airlines livery did not change on the SPs prior to their transfer to Mandarin: a white upper fuselage with a bare metal (now painted gray) hull, and a blue (upper) and red (lower) cheatline. The two stripes are also brought up the fin, where a Taiwan flag and registration number are placed. China Airlines titles in English and Chinese are painted in blue. The registration number is also located on the forward fuselage, below the cheatline.

Government of Saudi Arabia and Saudia–Saudi Arabian Airlines

Although the Saudi Royal Flight is a division of Saudi Arabian Airlines, Boeing's records reflect them as separate entities. The first SP delivered to the Kingdom (HZ-HM1, ln 329/msn 21652) was also the first of the Special Performance line to be powered by Rolls Royce engines, as well as the first with a VIP interior. This luxurious aircraft was equipped with a complete medical center to care for the well being of King Khaled, who had a heart condition and wore a pacemaker. The SP was selected because of its ability to quickly fly from Saudi Arabia to the King's specialist in Cleveland, Ohio, while allowing the medical staff on board to care for the King plus send real-time readouts of his condition via telemetry equipment to the hospital.

HZ-HM1 was ordered on November 9, 1977, and delivered on July 11, 1979. Lavishly furnished, it continues to serve the Royal

A beautiful view of third and final 747SP delivered to Saudi Arabia. HZ-AIJ (ln 560/msn 22750) is one of only six Rolls Royce-powered SPs. This aircraft was transferred from Saudia to the Saudi Royal Flight on October 1, 1992. (The Boeing Company Archives)

Family on flights throughout the world. A larger and even more spectacular 747-3G1 was delivered to King Fahd in December 1983, as HZ-HM1A (ln 592/msn 23070), and the SP was re-registered HZ-HM1B on September 30, 1984.

Two 747SPs (HZ-AIF, ln 529/msn 22503, and HZ-AIJ, ln 560/msn 22750) were ordered for use by Saudia–Saudi Arabian Airlines. HZ-AIF was ordered on December 19, 1979, and delivered on June 23, 1981. Nonstop service from Jeddah to New York began on July 2. Frequency was later increased to four flights per week, and a nonstop was also added from Dhahran to New York. The second SP was ordered in March 1981, and handed over on May 25, 1982. These Rolls Royce-equipped aircraft served the longest routes in the Saudia system until the advent of the 747-400. Because of its diminished role in carrying passengers, HZ-AIJ was transferred to Saudi Royal Flight on October 1, 1992, for conversion to a VIP aircraft.

Saudia HZ-AIF (ln 529/msn 22503) in flight. This view provides a better look at the barrel-shaped Rolls Royce RB.211-524BC engine nacelles. (Author's Collection)

The livery of the Royal Flight aircraft varies little from the Saudia passenger aircraft. All carried a white upper fuselage; a multi-hued cheatline with stripes of medium and dark green, white, and dark and medium blue; and a dark green tail with insignia and Saudia titles in white (tail titles are not applied to Royal Flight aircraft). Black fuselage titles for airline service, starboard side, read Saudi Arabian Airlines in English and Saudia in Arabic. The opposite appeared on the port side. Royal Flight aircraft fuselage titles simply read Saudia in both languages.

A new livery made its debut in early 1997, with a beige upper fuselage, gold trimline, white hull and engines; and a deep blue and turquoise tail with gold insignia. The titles Saudi Arabian appear in English and Arabic on both sides.

Braniff International Airways

Certainly one of the most colorful airlines in the sky, Braniff chose an orange livery for all four 747SP aircraft ordered. Two SPs N603BN (ln 405/msn 21785) and N604BN (ln 413/msn 21786) were purchased on May 22, 1978. The total cost of the order, including spares was $97.5 million. The aircraft were delivered on October 30, 1979, and April 23, 1980. The acquisition of the first two SPs doubled the size of Braniff's 747 fleet. N606BN (ln 447/msn 21992) was ordered on December 18, 1978, along with two additional 747-200Bs for $155 million. The third SP was delivered on May 30, 1980.

The fourth aircraft, N1608B (ln 473/msn 22302), was produced but not taken up, and later purchased by CAAC.

Braniff purchased these aircraft for their trans-Pacific service which included Los Angeles-to-Hong Kong via Guam or Seoul, and Atlanta to Honolulu via Dallas. The SPs were also scheduled to work a new Dallas–Bahrain route. Braniff's hasty over-expansion, higher fuel prices, and lower traffic due to an economic recession led to canceling all Pacific routes (except Dallas–Honolulu), and eventually to the end of operations, on May 13, 1982. But even before that time, Braniff had begun disposing of its large aircraft. All

Engaging the thrust reversers on Braniff International Airways' first SP, N603BN (ln 405/msn 21785). The big orange aircraft of Braniff were even more vivid on the inside, with bold, multihued panel patterns, and several colorful shades of leather on the seating surfaces throughout the aircraft. (The Boeing Company Archives)

three SPs were eventually sold. The first went back to Boeing and was parked until being purchased and refurbished for the government of Oman. N604BN was purchased by Aerolineas Argentinas, and N606BN was sold to Pan American.

The livery did not change during the SP's period of service with Braniff. Each remained all orange with pale yellow and fine gold stripes on the fin and around the orange engine nacelles. "Braniff International" titles were also in the same pale yellow.

N603BN undergoing final construction in the Everett Division plant. (The Boeing Company Archives)

Trans World Airlines

TWA ordered three 747SPs on October 17, 1978, in anticipation of opening new routes to the Middle East. When this service was not authorized, the aircraft were used on more conventional trans-continental and trans-Atlantic services. The aircraft were fitted with the optional exit door for seating 32 economy-class passengers on the upper deck. The coach seats were installed but removed prior to delivery and replaced with 12 first-class sleeper seats.

Delivery of the aircraft were made in the following order: N57202 (ln 439/msn 21962) on March 21, 1980, N58201 (ln 415/msn 21961) on April 14, 1980, and N57203 (ln 441/msn 21963) handed over on May 8, 1980. Each seated 290 passengers; 31 first-class main and upper deck sleeper seats and 259 economy-class. The straight staircase option was selected, as were the traditional transverse galleys. Nine main deck and two upper deck lavatories were installed.

Without the expected extra-long-range routes the aircraft were intended to fly, the SPs became redundant in a fleet of L-1011s and full-size 747s. One by one, they were disposed of. N57202 was sold on July 24, 1984, to become a VIP aircraft with the government of Brunei. This deal was not completed and later the SP migrated to American Airlines as N601AA. N58201 was transferred on February 22, 1985, to the government of Dubai, where it serves as VIP-configured aircraft A6-SMR. The last TWA SP (N57203) also went to American Airlines, as N602AA.

TWA's livery remained constant throughout the 747SP's short service history with the airline. It featured an all-white fuselage with twin red stripes; bold "Trans World" titles in red on the upper fuselage, and white TWA lettering surrounded by a red field on the tail.

Number two SP for Trans World Airlines, N57202 (ln 439/msn 21962), is taxied out to the runway at Paine Field. TWA ordered the additional capacity upper deck seating arrangement (see page 66) and has the required second emergency exit door just aft of the cockpit. (The Boeing Company Archives)

55

Civil Aviation Authority of China

The government of the People's Republic of China signed an agreement with Boeing for three 747SP jetliners on December 19, 1978. The order, approved by the China National Machinery Import and Export Corporation, specified delivery of the three aircraft to the Civil Aviation Authority of China (CAAC) in 1980. E.H. Boullioun, President of the Boeing Commercial Airplane Company, said, "We are extremely pleased that the airline of China has joined the ranks of 747 customers," and noted that, "The 747s will assist the People's Republic in realizing its commerce and tourism potential."

Actual handover of aircraft took place on February 26 (B-2442, ln 433/msn 21932), June 26 (B-2444, ln 455/msn 21933) and September 23 (N1304E, ln 467/msn 21934). The CAAC SPs were outfitted for 291 passengers, 30 first-class and 261 economy, and had Pratt and Whitney JT9D-7J engines rated at 50,000 pounds of thrust each. The order was the first from China since the historic purchase of ten 707 airliners on September 12, 1972.

Four CAAC flight crews received their 747 training at Boeing's flight simulator facilities in Seattle and completed their training in Beijing. The crews delivering B-2442 had plenty of time to get comfortable with their new SP during the 6,866-mile nonstop flight from Paine Field, Everett, Washington, to Beijing International Airport. The plane entered regular service a month later on April 2, 1980, with a flight from Beijing to Paris. The third SP, N1304E, made an intermediate stop on its delivery flight from Everett to Shanghai. CAAC's first revenue service from the U.S. departed from Seattle-Tacoma International Airport on October 1, 1980, as part of a General Motors Corp. sales incentive program. The round-trip charter flight was one of six authorized by the American government. Scheduled SP service was expanded from Beijing to London, Tokyo, and New York (by way of San Francisco). The SPs are also used for regional service within Asia.

A fourth SP (N1301E, ln 473/msn 22302), was added on June 15, 1983. Originally built for Braniff International Airways, N1608B was not taken up due to the carrier's grave financial condition. CAAC agreed to purchase the aircraft on December 23, 1982. The Chinese aircraft retained the American registration for almost six years, until it was changed to B-2454 on January 1, 1989.

The Chinese equivalent of airline deregulation took place on July 1, 1988, when CAAC was divided into several regional carriers. All four SPs were transferred on that date to the new international carrier Air China. All aircraft are currently in service.

The CAAC livery was fairly simple, with a white upper fuselage over a gray hull, a thin blue trim line above the blue cheatline. A small CAAC logo was placed on the forward fuselage above the cheatline. Black Chinese characters were also above the cheatline on the center fuselage, as was the large black registration number. A huge, swept-back flag dominated the plain-white fin. The base for the Air China livery is exactly the same as CAAC's livery. A small flag and Air China titles appear on the forward fuselage, the Chinese characters and registration number remain in the same location, and a large, red, stylized bird graces the tail.

The first wide-body jetliner for the People's Republic of China, B-2442 (ln 433/msn 21932), on the ramp in Beijing following its nonstop delivery flight from Everett. The aircraft entered commercial service on April 2, 1980, on a flight from Beijing to Paris. (Museum of Flight Archives)

Korean Air Lines

Two SPs were ordered by this fast-growing Asian airline, on April 10, 1979. HL7456 (ln 501/msn 22483) was delivered on January 22, 1981, and HL7457 (ln 507/msn 22484) followed two months later, on March 18. The new aircraft enabled Korean Air Lines (KAL) to greatly improve its service. Seoul-to-New York, previously flown via Anchorage with its 747-200s, could now be reached nonstop. The capitals of Europe and Asia were served by the versatile SPs until they were superseded by the larger 747-400s.

A three-class cabin layout is featured, with 12 upper-deck first-class seats; 40 "Prestige Class" (business-class) seats in Zones A and B, and 200 economy-class seats in the two rear cabins. Like most SP operators, KAL opted for the side-mounted galley.

The delivery colors were clean and simple, with a white upper fuselage; blue cheatline and thin red trim line; a large red flash on the tail, along with the KAL insignia also in red. Bold black Korean Air Lines titles were located on the center fuselage, followed by the same in Korean characters.

In 1984, the airline received a new name – Korean Air – and an attractive new look. The top of the fuselage was painted light blue, a thick silver cheatline was applied just below the windows, and the hull is white. The titles are in dark blue; with a round red, white,

A close-up shot of the first of two 747SPs for Korean Air Lines, HL7456 (ln 501/msn 22483). The Korean SPs were first used on the nonstop Seoul–New York route. (The Boeing Company Archives)

and blue insignia called the *Taeguk* on the tail and in place of the "o" in Korean. Similar to the national emblem on the South Korean flag, the red representing heaven, white progress and blue symbolizing the Earth. Indispensable to the Korean Air fleet for many years, the two SPs are now listed for sale.

Qantas

The first of two 747SP aircraft (VH-EAA, ln 505/msn 22495) was ordered by Qantas, along with three 747-200Bs and one full-size Combi model on January 16, 1980. The second (VH-EAB, ln 537/msn 22672) was ordered six months later. The SPs were delivered on January 19 and August 31, 1981, and used primarily on the Sydney-to-Los Angeles nonstop service, until replaced by new 747-400s. They were also briefly used on flights to Wellington, New Zealand, where they were the ideal high-capacity aircraft for that city's short runway and the local terrain.

Both SPs were transferred to Qantas subsidiary Australia Asia Airlines for service between Sydney and Taipei. This was necessary because of restrictions placed by the government of the People's Republic of China. When Qantas privatized in 1995, flying the

A five-engined SP? The 747 has the optional capability to ferry a spare power plant from one base to another. The engine, which is complete except for the fan blades, is mounted under the left wing as shown. A nose cowl, fan cowl and forward strut fairing are provided to streamline the spare engine kit. Qantas also made use of the extra engine pod option for its 707 aircraft. This SP is shown with Boeing registration N1791B during testing. It was delivered as VH-EAB *Winton* (ln 537/msn 22672) on August 31, 1981. (Boeing Commercial Airplane Group)

The Original Boeing SP?

Qantas 707-138B VH-EBH (ln 201/msn 18067) was delivered on July 29, 1961. The standard 707 fuselage was shortened by 10 feet to reduce weight and improve range for long overseas flights (the -138B was also 1 foot, 8 inches shorter than the 720). Unlike the 747SP, which can fly nonstop from Sydney to San Francisco, the 707-138B required stops in Fiji and Honolulu. Qantas – the first non-U.S. airline to operate the 707 – was also the only carrier to order this version of the 707. Named *City of Darwin*, VH-EBH was the first new B-model delivered to the Australian airline; other 707-138s in the Qantas fleet were later modified to -138B standards. (The Boeing Company Archives)

Taipei route no longer had the same political implications, and it started service to Taiwan under the Qantas name.

The SPs were repainted in Qantas liveries in June and August 1995 and resumed flying on a variety of routes in the South Pacific and Asia. Both aircraft are 5th-pod-certified to carry a spare Rolls Royce RB.211-524D4 engine (while testing the pod configuration VH-EAB carried Boeing test registration N1791B). The interiors are configured to carry 20 Zone A business-class passengers and 292 coach-class, main and upper deck seats, and the longitudinal galley. Qantas plans to retain both aircraft for service into the foreseeable future.

The delivery colors for Qantas featured a white upper fuselage with an orange cheatline and titles with Qantas in red and Australia in orange, separated with the letters "SP" in red and white stripes which almost looked pink from a distance. The tail was red with the trademark flying kangaroo in white. Large white SP letters were also placed on the tip of the fin. The aircraft names *City of Gold Coast-Tweed* (-EAA), and *Winton* (-EAB) were carried on the forward fuselage, below the cheatline.

Qantas updated to a new "Euro-white" look which sports red tail colors that continue around the fuselage at the same angle as the leading edge of the fin. A fine gold trim line separates the red from the white of the main fuselage. The white kangaroo (now without wings) extends from the tail onto the fuselage. Qantas titles, in black, are applied between the Number One and Number Two entry doors, just above the window line; with "The Spirit of Australia" below the window line. Name location reamains in the same place on the fuselage. Australia Asia retained the same look as Qantas, replacing the kangaroo with two stylized "ribbons" flashing across the red tail. Australia Asia titles were centered under the upper-deck windows, with the name repeated in Chinese characters below.

Iraqi Airways

YI-ALM (ln 567/msn 22858) was ordered by Iraqi Airways, but transferred immediately upon delivery to the Iraqi government on August 30, 1982, for service as a VIP aircraft. The SP features a complete VIP interior, with stateroom, conference room, and a lounge with sleeper seats. Painted in Iraqi Airways' dark green and medium green colors, the airplane carries "Iraq" titles rather than Iraqi Airways (Koufai script on the port side and English on the starboard side). The Iraqi Airways logo, but not the titles, was applied to the tail.

YI-ALM has been parked and in storage in Tozeur, Tunisia, since January 1991, due to the Gulf War and subsequent no-fly restrictions. It was painted all white for protection from desert heat. The name *Al Qadissiya* appears above the cheatline on the forward fuselage.

Iraqi Government 747SP YI-ALM (ln 567/msn 22858) shown here at McGuire Air Force Base, New Jersey, in September 1989. This aircraft featured a complete VIP interior. During the Gulf War, it was ferried to Tozeur, Tunisia, for protective storage and remains grounded in an all-white livery. Because of the no-fly restrictions in Iraq, the future of YI-ALM is uncertain. (Barry Roop via Maurice Bertrand)

Government of Abu Dhabi

A luxurious VIP aircraft, A6-ZSN (ln 676/msn 23610) flies for the United Arab Emirates/Abu Dhabi Amiri Flight. The final 747SP off the assembly line, it took almost 30 months to furnish the elaborate interior and install state-of-the-art electronic equipment. It was one of only six SPs equipped with Rolls Royce engines and has a distinctive dome for satellite communications mounted on the upper deck. Finally completed, the SP was handed over on December 9, 1989, in Vancouver, British Columbia. The livery with its all-white fuselage and engines, red cheatline, and large flag on the fin has not changed since delivery.

The 45th and final 747SP off the production line. The government of Abu Dhabi's SP A6-ZSN (ln 676/msn 23610), shown here in temporary registration N60697, was delivered over seven years after handover of the Iraqi SP. Costs incurred to restart SP production must have been enormous, but when one considers the financial condition of the buyer, it seems apparent that money was not an overwhelming factor. (Jean-Luc Altherr via Jan Mogren)

Chapter VIII
Inside the 747SP

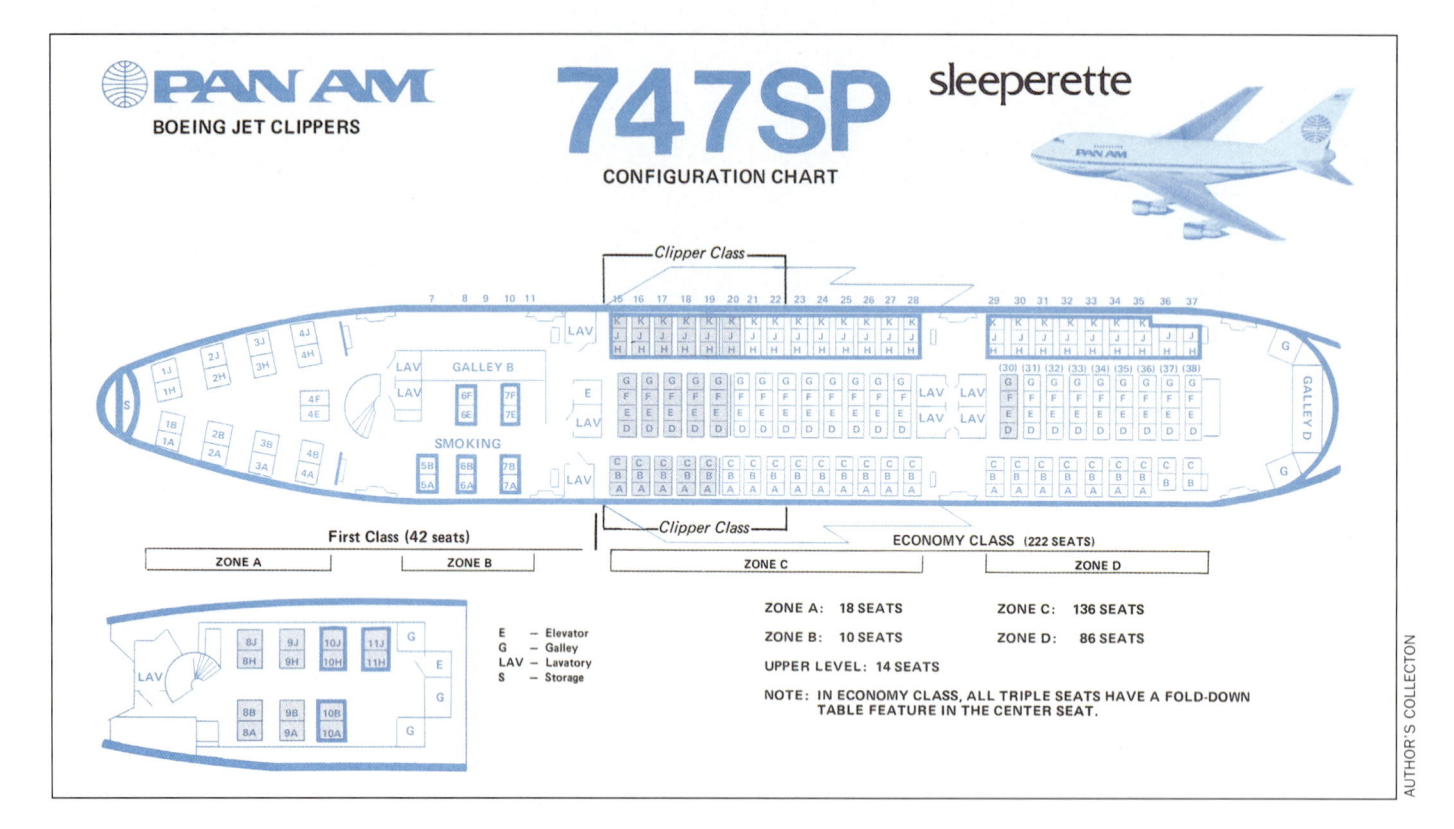

The general layout of the 747SP is basically the same as the standard 747, featuring a 20-foot-wide cabin, an upper deck accessible by a staircase, and thousands of cubic feet of cargo space below. The main difference of course is its length. The cabin in the SP is 138 feet, 8 inches, compared to 187 feet in the standard 747. The main deck is divided into zones by the four pairs of entry doors. Zone A is usually reserved for first-class passengers, Zone B can be configured for additional first-class, a business-class section or the beginning of the coach compartment. Zones C and D are the main coach-class cabins. The upper deck, once used as a first-class lounge, is now reserved for more lucrative first-, business- or coach-class seating. Inflight meal service is prepared in either the SP's forward longitudinal galley or in the more traditional transverse galleys, as well as in the aft main deck galley. The upper deck also has its own galley with a cart lift to improve service for those passengers. At least nine main deck lavatories were available for passengers, plus one upstairs.

The airlines selected the cabin furnishings, colors and materials for their aircraft. These could vary from conservative styles and colors as were selected by TWA, with its cream colored leather in first class and simple gray, blue and red cloth in coach. Braniff International went on a completely opposite course with bold, '70s-style, eye-popping colors throughout the aircraft. Leather seats in all cabins and panels in waves of purple, orange, yellow, turquoise and blue. Korean Air Lines chose somewhere more in the middle for its first 747SP designs, selecting a comfortable and elegant brown leather for the first-class seats but livening up coach with multi-hued designs of bright greens, reds, oranges and golds. Cabin panels featured loud colors and Korean designs. CAAC chose a more traditional approach for its cabin. Subtle Chinese art was applied to the main bulkhead surfaces. Seats were covered in cloth with simple patterns and muted shades of blue, orange and green. For its first SPs, the "other" China (China Airlines) selected rich reds and golds for first-class and colorful orange, blue and reds for the main cabins. The China Airlines upper deck lounge was truly a sight to behold. Pan American was very "current" with its colors, selecting bright reds and deep blues for first-class and a variety of orange, gold and blue for coach.

The photographs on the following pages provide a "zone-by-zone" look at the interiors of the 747SP, including the several upper deck configurations, various galley designs, the flight deck, and the cargo hold. These photographs were taken aboard new aircraft, prior to delivery, by The Boeing Company.

Above: Zone A. The main-deck first-class seating area aboard Pan American SP N533PA (ln 273/msn 21025). This forward cabin section offered deluxe, nonsmoking accommodations for 18 passengers. The bulkhead graphics continued the Pan Am "Clipper" theme which was evident throughout the first-class section. Zone A is free from service equipment and lavatories, offering a quiet environment for the passengers. (The Boeing Company Archives)

Below: Zone B. CAAC chose to maximize the use of this section by seating 30 economy-class passengers between the Number One and Number Two entry doors. Aircraft B-2442 (ln 433/msn 21932) featured this lovely Chinese mountain scene on the four panels opposite the longitudinal galley. Screens in other SPs flying in the CAAC fleet featured a bamboo forest motif (B-2444) and a flock of geese in formation above the clouds (N1304E). (The Boeing Company Archives)

Above: Zone C. TWA selected conservative fabrics and panel designs for the interiors of their SP fleet. The largest SP cabin section could accommodate 148 economy-class passengers. The aircraft shown is N57202 (ln 439/msn 21962) TWA also chose a more traditional cabin layout, installing two forward transverse galleys rather than the longitudinal galley option. (The Boeing Company Archives)

Below: Zone D. To complement its vivid exteriors, Braniff International Airways designers chose a bright spectrum of interior colors. Seats were covered in leather throughout all cabin sections, including the 82 economy seats in Zone D. Single lavatory compartments were installed behind the last row of seats on the cabin wall. The SP's aft galley arrangement allowed crews to work in privacy, away from lavatory traffic. The photo shows the interior of N603BN (ln 405/msn 21785). (The Boeing Company Archives)

Right: Looking down the spiral staircase of Syrianair SP YK-AHA (ln 284/msn 21174). Beginning in early 1976, an optional, redesigned L-shaped stairway permitted easier access for upper deck passengers. The narrow stairs on the spiral staircase were notorious for tripping up passengers and flight crew alike. (The Boeing Company Archives)

Below: The improved "straight" stairway aboard South African Airways ZS-SPD (ln 293/msn 21253). Access to the longitudinal galley is curtained off behind the row of seats on the left. A mini-galley is directly below the stairs, opposite two first-class lavatories. (The Boeing Company Archives)

63

Above: The upper deck first-class lounge aboard Pan American SP N533PA (ln 273/msn 21025). At mealtime, the lounge was transformed into a dining room resplendent in white linen, polished silverware and fine china. Behind the red curtain was a galley (see page 67), which supplied access to everything the upper deck passengers required. Transparent panels featured clipper ships in keeping with Pan Am tradition. Forward of the staircase was a single lavatory and the flight deck. (The Boeing Company Archives)

Below: The exotic upper deck lounge of Iran Air EP-IAA (ln 275/msn 20998). This truly first-class lounge featured a large, polished brass samovar (water boiler and teapot warmer). Despite appearances, this was not your usual Iranian samovar. To meet FAA inflight requirements, the urn had to survive being subjected to nine Gs (or nine times the force of gravity). The electrically operated samovar had a stainless steel water-container insert and control lights to help the cabin attendant maintain proper water level for both tea preparation and aircraft movement. (The Boeing Company Archives)

Above: In China the color red signifies luck, so those in the upper deck lounge of China Airlines SP B-1862 (ln 304/msn 21300) could feel very fortunate, indeed. This stunning "palace of the air" once seated 15 first-class passengers. In keeping with the theme, the galley was also finished in red. (The Boeing Company Archives)

Below: CAAC SP B-2442 (ln 433/msn 21932) offered upper deck sleeper seats for its first-class passengers. The large seats were finished in subtle green cloth, providing understated elegance. (The Boeing Company Archives)

Above: Qantas set a new standard for upper deck luxury aboard VH-EAA (ln 505/msn 22495). The 12 extra-wide and plush first-class sleeper seats allowed passengers a comfortable way to pass the many miles on the way to Australia. Woodgrained stowage bins were placed below the windows for passenger convenience. (The Boeing Company Archives)

Below: A short-lived configuration aboard the TWA SPs. The 32-seat economy-class upper deck layout was replaced by 12 first-class sleeper seats prior to entering passenger service. This aircraft, N57202 (ln 439/msn 21962) began revenue flying on April 22, 1980. (The Boeing Company Archives)

Left: The innovative SP longitudinal galley. Designed to allow simultaneous service to first-class and forward-cabin coach passengers, this design also permitted servicing of the galley without interfering with the loading or unloading of passengers. A special epoxy finish floor incorporated raised sills to keep liquid spills in the galley area for easy cleanup. A row of 11, six-wheel service carts made loading and unloading of trays quicker and easier. Three double "TIA" ovens, with stainless steel doors, are pictured in the center of the galley. Each oven contained four cookie sheets, with each sheet holding up to seven entrees. There was plenty of storage above the ovens and in overhead compartments. The galley pictured is aboard CAAC SP B-2442 (ln 433/msn 21932). (The Boeing Company Archives)

Below: The upper deck galley aboard Korean Air Lines SP HL7456 (ln 501/msn 22483). For multiple meal service flights and duty-free service, it was necessary to switch used and unused carts between the main deck and upper deck galleys. This was accomplished by using the cart lift (rust colored door with window, to the lower left of the center galley). A safety lock allowed the door to be opened only when the lift was positioned at the door. The panel for operating the elevator is at the top of the bulkhead, directly above the lift door. (The Boeing Company Archives)

67

Above: The standard transverse style main deck galley aboard the Iraqi government 747SP YI-ALM (ln 567/msn 22858). Located between the number two entry doors, this galley was one of two serving the forward section of the aircraft. It contained six modular carts and two double ovens. A lounge area can be partially seen forward of the galley. (The Boeing Company Archives)

Below: The aft main deck galley provided a spacious work area for food preparation. Like the longitudinal configuration, the location of the aft galley allowed crews to work without lavatory traffic interference and permitted the galley to be serviced on the ground from aft entry doors while passengers were boarding at the opposite end of the aircraft. Twelve serving carts and three double ovens expedited the process of serving passengers in Zones C and D. Pictured is the galley from Syrianair YK-AHA (ln 284/msn 21174). (The Boeing Company Archives)

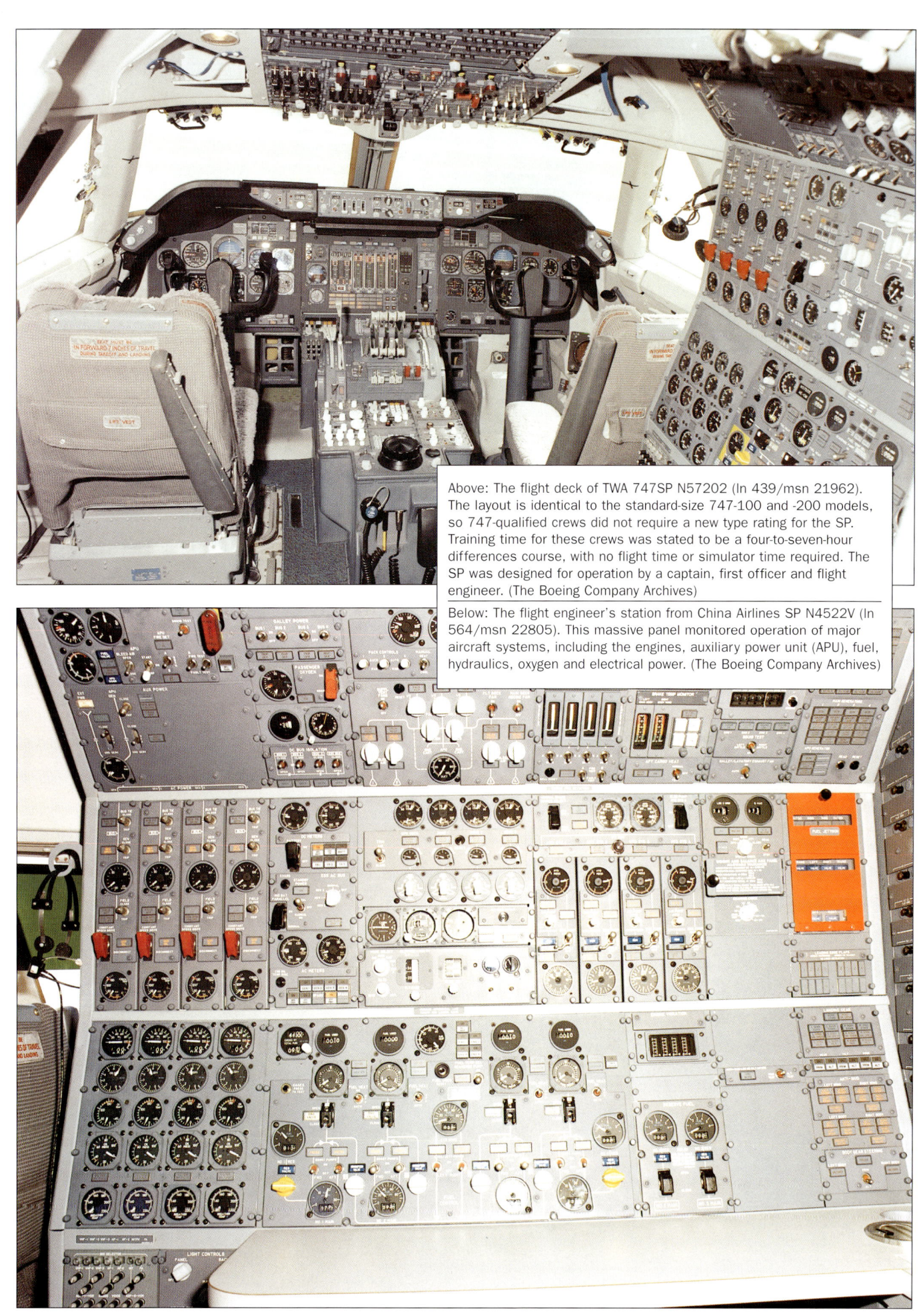

Above: The flight deck of TWA 747SP N57202 (ln 439/msn 21962). The layout is identical to the standard-size 747-100 and -200 models, so 747-qualified crews did not require a new type rating for the SP. Training time for these crews was stated to be a four-to-seven-hour differences course, with no flight time or simulator time required. The SP was designed for operation by a captain, first officer and flight engineer. (The Boeing Company Archives)

Below: The flight engineer's station from China Airlines SP N4522V (ln 564/msn 22805). This massive panel monitored operation of major aircraft systems, including the engines, auxiliary power unit (APU), fuel, hydraulics, oxygen and electrical power. (The Boeing Company Archives)

Above: The upper deck crew rest area aboard South African Airways SP ZS-SPD (ln 293/msn 21253). Located in a small compartment behind the flight deck, the rest area offered crew members an opportunity to stretch out on long flights. The simple accommodations included two bunks, ventilation, reading lights, and personal item storage pockets. Placards advised: "Occupy with head aft when using bunk" and "Bunk not to be occupied during takeoff and landing." (The Boeing Company Archives)

Below: The aft lower deck cargo compartment of Pan American SP N533PA (ln 273/msn 21025). This photograph was taken from the back of the compartment, facing forward. In the basic configuration, each of the two lower cargo holds could accommodate up to 10 LD-1 half-width containers for a total of 3,460 cubic feet. The aft compartment also had room for an additional 400 cubic feet of bulk cargo space. (The Boeing Company Archives)

Chapter IX
747SP Pictorial History

The author has attempted to present a visual history of all 45 Boeing 747SP aircraft by providing a collection of photographs that represent the broadest possible selection of airline and government liveries, including some unusual, temporary markings. Because of space limitations, it is not possible to show every variation of every aircraft. The following photographs are presented in order by aircraft line number (LN), which represents production sequence. Also shown is the manufacturer's serial number (MSN).

An exceptional overhead view of Australia Asia SP VH-EAA (ln 505/msn 22495), showing the enormous wingspan and the short, wide fuselage. (Julian Green)

LN 265/MSN 21022

Decked out in a patriotic red, white and blue livery for its Independence Day first flight, N747SP was the first of 45 Special Performance 747s built. (The Boeing Company Archives)

N530PA Clipper Mayflower. The first five Pan Am SP aircraft were given names in honor of the American Bicentennial. (Terry Waddington)

When Pan Am's Pacific routes were sold to United Airlines, the largest fleet of SPs was included in the transaction. N140UA is pictured at San Francisco with large United titles. (Maurice Bertrand)

LN 268/MSN 21023

N247SP *Clipper Liberty Bell* on the ramp at Everett. It was one of three SPs involved in the FAA certification program. The test aircraft logged almost 545 hours on 340 flights – with no major design or mechanical problems found. (The Boeing Company Archives)

Transition time for N531PA A very tired looking SP carries new United titles and an old Pan Am registration number while waiting for a trip to the paint hangar. (John Kitchen via Jim Thompson)

Bright and shiny in United markings and distinctive white nacelles, N141UA departs for yet another trans-Pacific journey. (Maurice Bertrand)

LN 270/MSN 21024

Clipper Constitution is seen on her maiden flight over the city of Mount Vernon, Washington. The third SP built, it would be the first fitted with a passenger interior. (Museum of Flight Archives)

Now registered N532PA, *Clipper Constitution* awaits a new load of passengers. (Terry Waddington)

N532PA changes hands. The Pan Am stripe, registration number and flag on the fin are still intact, but the Pan Am titles and "Clipper" name have been covered up by the new owners. (Bill Hough)

Lighter in weight, but with the same powerful 747 engines, the SP is famous for hot takeoffs. N142UA already has the gear stowed and is speeding its way up to a comfortable 41,000-foot cruising altitude. (Jim Thompson Collection)

LN 273/MSN 21025

Beautiful view of the fourth SP built, which highlights the underside of the aircraft. This angle clearly shows the SPs severely tapered aft fuselage, extended stabilizer and tail. N40135 is shown here during some of its 15 hours of flight testing before leaving on the 72,152-mile demonstration tour. (The Boeing Company Archives)

N533PA *Clipper Freedom* was the first 747SP to be delivered to Pan American. Immediately after handover, the aircraft was ferried to Seattle-Tacoma International Airport to take aboard a load of cargo for shipment to New York. The new SP dwarfs Pan Am 707-321B *Clipper Norwester*. (The Boeing Company Archives)

New look for a veteran world traveler. N533PA, now named *Clipper Young America*, sports Pan Am's "Billboard" livery and a commemorative "Flight 50" sticker. A historic, trailblazing aircraft, N533PA was a veteran of Boeing's worldwide demonstration tour and two record-setting round-the-world flights. (ATP/Airliners America)

N143UA with United, on final approach to London-Heathrow. Sadly, this great aircraft was one of five United SPs broken up for spares. Its legacy lives on, however, with numerous entries in aviation record books. (Avion Foto by Jay Selman)

LN 275/MSN 20988

The first SP for Iran Air also has the distinction of carrying the lowest SP serial number. EP-IAA *Kurdistan*, shown here in Geneva in July 1983. (Maurice Bertrand collection)

LN 278/MSN 20999

Iran Air EP-IAB *Khorasan*, handed over on May 10, 1976. Three of the four Iranian SPs have retained the same basic livery since delivery. (Maurice Bertrand)

LN 280/MSN 21132

ZS-SPA *Matroosberg*, the first of six SPs purchased by South African Airways, would break the distance record for commercial aircraft on its delivery flight to Johannesburg. (The Boeing Company)

Air Mauritius 3B-NAJ *Chateau Mon Plaisir*, was leased for seven years while serving on nonstop flights from the Indian Ocean island nation to Europe. The SPs were replaced by Airbus A-340-300s, which provide substantially better economy than the older jet. (Jan Mogren Collection)

Distinctive colors of Alliance Airlines, registered as ZS-SPA. Truly an alliance, the airline was organized by Air Tanzania, Air Uganda and South African Airways to expand air traffic into East Africa. Service to London and the Middle East began in July 1995, using this aircraft leased from SAA. (via Eddy Gual)

LN 282/MSN 21133

ZS-SPB shown here in original SAA livery. The starboard side carried the South African Airways titles in Afrikaans and the port side in English. This aircraft bore the name *Outeniqua*. (Terry Waddington Collection)

A widely photographed view of Air Malawi 7Q-YKL. Leased from South African Airways from April 12 to May 11, 1985, the SP was given standard Air Malawi titles and tail markings (retaining the blue SAA cheatline). The sole purpose of the short-term lease was to transport President Hastings Banda to Britain for an official visit. The aircraft, named *Mulanje*, was parked in this location at Heathrow for three weeks before being returned to SAA. (Tommy Mogren Collection)

Luxair made two unsuccessful attempts to establish service from Luxembourg to Johannesburg with aircraft obtained from South African Airways. In November 1987, Luxair leased ZS-SPB, had it painted in its colors and re-registered the SP as LX-LGX. It remained in Luxair service for nearly six years, flying a 307-seat all-economy configuration. (Eric LeGendre via Terry Waddington)

Trek Airways of South Africa leased ZS-SPB for a seven-month period from September 1993 to April 1994. (Tommy Mogren Collection)

Air Namibia leased ZS-SPB from South African Airways for service on its popular nonstop Windhoek-to-Europe routes. (Jan Mogren Collection)

LN 284/MSN 21174

YK-AHA of Syrianair approaching London-Heathrow. Delivered on May 21, 1976, the SP has provided dependable service on medium-range routes to Europe and the Middle East from Damascus. This aircraft was christened *November 16*. (Avion Foto by Jay Selman)

LN 286/MSN 21026

Pan Am *Clipper Great Republic* N534PA, photographed at Los Angeles International. The SPs established the longest of Pan Am's numerous routes to Asia, the South Pacific, and the Middle East. (Terry Waddington Collection)

Head-on view of United's N144UA. An "SP" label was applied in front of the nose gear to identify the aircraft type for proper handling by ground crews. (Maurice Bertrand)

LN 288/MSN 21134

South African Airways ZS-SPC on climbout. This aircraft sports an updated livery with wider cheatlines, bolder fuselage titles and a larger "flying springbok" on the tail. The name *Maluti* appears on the forward fuselage. (Avion Foto by Jorg Zmich)

The first of five SPs operated by Air Mauritius replaced a Boeing 707 on its then-weekly service from Port Louis to London-Heathrow, cutting travel time on the long route to 14 hours. The name *Chateau de Reduit* appears on the forward fuselage below the trimline on 3B-NAG. (via Eddy Gual)

ZS-SPC *Gauteng*, was leased to South African carrier Avia in March 1995 and began operations the next month. Service was scheduled three times per week from Johannesburg to London-Gatwick. Only three months later, Avia had to suspend service and the aircraft was returned to South African Airways, a victim of its own deeply discounted fare structure. (Mike Axe)

LN 290/MSN 21175

Like its sister ship, the livery on Syrianair YK-AHB *Arab Solidarity* has not changed since delivery from Boeing in 1976.
(Terry Waddington collection)

LN 293/MSN 21253

ZS-SPD was the first South African Airways SP sold to another operator. Originally leased to Royal Air Maroc in March 1985, it was then purchased off lease 18 months later. During service with SAA, the aircraft carried the name *Majuba*. It is seen at Zurich in 1978.
(Jan Mogren Collection via Nicky Scherrer)

With Royal Air Maroc as CN-RMS, this SP was primarily used for service to North and South America from Casablanca. (Jon Proctor Collection)

83

French airline Corsair purchased CN-RMS to serve on its routes from Paris-Orly to Nouméa, New Caledonia and Papeete to Los Angeles or Oakland, California. The aircraft was originally registered in Luxembourg (as LX-ACO) because the SP was not certified in France. (Duncan Stewart via Maurice Bertrand)

Corsair's SP received French certification in November 1995, and was later re-registered as F-GTOM. The airline removed the original longitudinal galley and replaced it with the conventional transverse type to increase the seating capacity to around 350. (Eric M. Trum)

LN 298/MSN 21254

South African Airways christened its fifth SP, ZS-SPE *Hantam*. (Terry Waddington)

Leased to help the airline expand its international service until new aircraft could be received, 3B-NAR *Chateau Labourdonnais* joined the Air Mauritius fleet on November 1, 1991. (Tommy Mogren Collection)

Shown here with Air Namibia titles and registration, a white tail and a South African Airways cheatline, V5-SPE was painted in an interim livery from March 25 to May 12, 1993. The aircraft has since been returned to full SAA colors, with its original ZS-SPE registration.
(Bruce Drum Collection)

LN 301/MSN 21263

The sixth and last SP purchased by South African Airways, ZS-SPF was named *Soutpansberg* after a South African mountain peak. Like all of the SAA 747SPs, it has been leased out to several other airlines. (H.J. Schroeder via Terry Waddington)

Air Mauritius 3B-NAO photographed in an incomplete livery at Paris-Orly in October 1988. The tail carries only the stylized bird emblem; there is no Mauritius flag or aircraft name. (Jan Mogren Collection via Nicky Scherrer)

The all-white livery of LX-LGY with UTA titles. Leased for less than two months to the French airline, the aircraft was registered in Luxembourg. This photograph was taken on October 27, 1989. (Christian Volpati)

Less than a month after Namibia became an independent nation, Namib Air, the national airline, was flying a leased 747SP on the route to Frankfurt, Germany. The former South African Airways ZS-SPF was given a bright new white, yellow and blue livery, a new name – *Etosha* – and Namibian registration V5-SPF. (Terry Waddington Collection)

In 1991, the Namib Air titles were changed to Air Namibia, but the livery remained the same. (ATP/Airliners America)

LN 304/MSN 21300

B-1862 was the first of four SPs purchased by China Airlines to establish nonstop routes across the Pacific. Boeing used the aircraft to test access to the side fuselage for the possibility of building an SP Combi variant. (Tommy Mogren Collection)

A privately owned company formed by China Airlines, Mandarin Airlines operates flights to countries where Taiwan does not have diplomatic relations. Mandarin began service to Sydney, Australia, and Vancouver, B.C., in late 1991. (Maurice Bertrand)

LN 306/MSN 21441

N536PA Pan Am *Clipper Lindbergh* at Hong Kong's Kai Tak airport. The aircraft was christened by Anne Morrow Lindbergh to commemorate the 50th anniversary of her husband's solo trans-Atlantic flight. (The Boeing Company Archives)

Sharp looking in United's three-stripe livery, N145UA prepares to depart Los Angeles on a trans-Pacific flight. The small United titles were later replaced with larger examples. (Maurice Bertrand)

The only SP painted in United Airlines most recent gray/blue color scheme, N145UA shines in the afternoon sunlight. (Edwin Terbeek)

The SP's size and ability to make sustained flights to the edge of the Earth's atmosphere make it the perfect platform to carry a large telescope for NASA's Stratospheric Observatory For Infrared Astronomy (SOFIA) program. The black painted section on the aft fuselage will be the location of the opening for the telescope. (Ed Davies)

LN 307/MSN 21093

Iran Air's third SP, EP-IAC *Fars* arrives in London following a flight from Tehran in 1987. (Maurice Bertrand)

LN 325/MSN 21547

Pan Am *Clipper High Flyer* N537PA at JFK Airport, New York. This SP would also carry the name *Clipper Washington*. (Avion Foto by Jay Selman)

Awaiting clearance for takeoff at San Francisco International, United SP N146UA shows off its massive leading-edge slats. (Maurice Bertrand)

The remnants of United's colors fading in the Arizona sun, N146UA awaits a new buyer while in storage at Marana. (Bob Shane)

LN 329/MSN 21652

Right: A luxurious flying palace for King Khaled, HZ-HM1 was fitted with a complete medical center to care for the King, who had a heart condition. Saudi Royal Flight aircraft can be quickly distinguished by the lack of titles on the tail, and an abundance of antennae along the upper surfaces of the aircraft. (The Boeing Company Archives)

90

Preview of the new Saudi Arabian livery at Boeing Field, Seattle, on January 31, 1997. HZ-HM1B shows off the striking sand, blue and white colors during its brief visit. This was the first SP to be fitted with Rolls Royce engines. (Jeffrey S. DeVore)

LN 331/MSN 21548

In memory of an American-born Princess, Pan Am christened N538PA in honor of the late Grace Kelly. This photograph was taken in May 1985. (ATP/Airliners America)

N147UA flew around the world in record time as *Friendship One* in 1988. The aircraft still carries the name in this photograph taken at Sydney. (Tommy Mogren Collection)

In June 1993, United Airlines made the decision to retire 10 SPs and 15 McDonnell Douglas DC-10s. N146UA and N147UA (shown above) are stored in the dry desert air at Marana, Arizona. These are the last of the United SPs waiting to be placed with new owners. (Bob Shane)

LN 367/MSN 21648

Pan American 747SP *Clipper Black Hawk*, N539PA. The cheatline reflects a way to cut costs and improve appearances by stopping just short of the radome, avoiding mismatched stripes on the nose. (John Stewart via Nicholas A. Veronico)

After 15 years of carrying passengers with Pan American and United, N148UA was sold to Worldwide Aircraft Holding Company for conversion to a luxurious transport for the leadership of the government of Qatar. (ATP/Airliners America)

VR-BAT at London-Heathrow in January 1997. This VIP-configured aircraft is painted in the same maroon color as the Qatar flag. (SPA Photography via Tommy Mogren Collection)

LN 371/MSN 21758

Because of political problems with the Iranian government, the delivery of the fourth and final SP for Iran Air was done quietly and on neutral ground at Frankfurt, Germany. EP-IAD was handed over in plain white paint with no markings except for the registration number.
(Terry Waddington Collection)

The all-white look remains on EP-IAD. Bold titles and a large Homa Bird provide a welcome change from the aging delivery colors that remain on the first three Iranian SPs. (Avion Foto by Jonny Andersson)

LN 373/MSN 21649

N540PA was delivered May 11, 1979 as *Clipper White Falcon*. Pan American changed its name at least three more times, to *Clipper Flying Arrow*, *Clipper Star of the Union* and *China Clipper*. (Avion Foto by Jay Selman)

United Airlines retired 747SP N149UA in October 1993, and by late November it was leased to Tajik Air of the former Soviet Republic of Tajikistan. (Maurice Bertrand)

While flying as Tajik Air *Snow Leopard*, the aircraft retained its American registration (N149UA). The SP only remained with Tajik Air for 79 days and was returned to United. (Jan Mogren Collection)

N149UA was purchased for the government of Brunei and registered V8-JBB, V8-JP1, and finally V8-AC1. Painted in an attractive and distinctive livery, V8-AC1 is pictured at JFK on January 29, 1997. (Michael McLaughlin via Tommy Mogren Collection)

LN 405/MSN 21785

Braniff International Airways, after considering the McDonnell Douglas DC-10-30 and the Lockheed L-1011, ordered four SPs for South American and trans-Pacific services. The first, N603BN, is shown on a pre-delivery flight. (Museum of Flight Archives)

Purchased back by Boeing due to Braniff's financial problems, N603BN remained parked three years while waiting for a buyer. The government of Oman purchased the SP, re-registered it as A40-SO, and took another three years to have it configured as a VIP transport. The large dome houses satellite communications equipment. (Avion Foto Collection)

LN 413/MSN 21786

N604BN, second of the Braniff SPs, saw only five months of service with the Texas-based carrier before being sold to Aerolineas Argentinas. (Avion Foto by Jay Selman)

The only Aerolineas Argentinas SP, LV-OHV, takes off for Buenos Aires. It was flown on the South American airline's longest routes for almost 10 years. (Maurice Bertrand)

The five Air Mauritius SPs, including 3B-NAQ *Chateau Benares*, were utilized for approximately 10 hours daily until being gradually replaced by a new fleet of Boeing 767s and Airbus A340-300s. (Avion Foto by Roberto Farina)

3B-NAQ was purchased from Air Mauritius by Qatar Airways on February 8, 1996, then sold to the government of Qatar for VIP conversion. The aircraft, re-registered A7-AHM, is seen while undergoing major upgrades. (Bob Shane)

LN 415/MSN 21961

TWA ordered three 747SPs on October 17, 1978, in anticipation of new nonstop service to the Middle East. When the route authority was not approved, the aircraft, including N58201, were used on more standard routes not requiring the special performance abilities of the aircraft. (Terry Waddington)

Sold to the government of Dubai by TWA, A6-SMR was fitted with a luxury interior for service with the Royal Flight. (via Eddy Gual)

LN 433/MSN 21932

Delivered to Beijing on a nonstop 6,866-mile flight from Everett, Washington, CAAC 747SP B-2442 began the first wide-body passenger service for the People's Republic of China on April 2, 1980. (Maurice Bertrand collection)

B-2442 was transferred from CAAC to Air China on July 1, 1988. (via Eddy Gual)

LN 439/MSN 21962

N57202 saw only four years of service with Trans World prior to being sold. The SP had no extra-long-range routes to serve with TWA and became redundant in a wide-body fleet of standard-size 747s and L-1011s. (Avion Foto by Jay Selman)

Jet Aviation purchased N57202 for a planned VIP conversion and delivery to the government of Brunei. When this project was not completed, the aircraft was sold – along with N57203 – to American Airlines. (John Kitchen via Jim Thompson)

N601AA at Marana, Arizona, in preparation for delivery to American Airlines. Along with N602AA (ln 441/msn 21963), the SPs were gutted and had completely new interiors installed. The bare metal exterior was buffed to perfection. (Jon Proctor)

Kazakhstan Airlines *Sunkar*. Flagship of the fledgling airline, the SP's upper deck was configured for use as a luxurious stateroom for President Nursultan Nazarbaev. Despite the presidential role of the aircraft, the lower deck was configured for use as a standard commercial airliner. (The Boeing Company Archives)

99

Returned after two years of service to the owner, the Kazakhstan Airlines SP was converted to a full VIP interior for use by the government of Brunei. Shown here at Newark, New Jersey, in February 1997, the aircraft still carries the fine blue Kazakhstan trimline. (A.J. Smith)

LN 441/MSN 21963

TWA's N57203 at John F. Kennedy International. As of June 3, 1985, TWA was offering this SP for sale at $37 million. The aircraft went to American Airlines as N602AA. (Jon Proctor)

N57203 in bare metal at Marana, Arizona. A small portion of the TWA colors remain behind the wing. American required the SP's ultra-long range to fly its newly awarded nonstop Dallas-to-Tokyo route. The nose of N601AA can be seen in the background. (John Adkins)

In 1990, when TWA sold several of its trans-Atlantic London routes to American Airlines for $445 million, American moved both of its SPs from the Pacific routes to New York-London service. N602AA began operations with American on May 21, 1987. (Jim Thompson)

Purchased by the government of Dubai from American Airlines on April 7, 1994, A6-SMM would require 10 months to transition to VIP service. Photographed in Geneva, June 1995. (Max Fankhauser via Jan Mogren Collection)

LN 445/MSN 22298

China Airlines B-1880 was delivered April 30, 1980. The SP was well-suited to fly the airline's growing long-distance routes from Taipei. (Akinobu Okuda via Maurice Bertrand)

B-1880 in Mandarin Airlines colors, at San Francisco International Airport. Mandarin is Taiwan's third international carrier. (Edwin Terbeek)

LN 447/MSN 21992

Part of a huge 747 buying spree, N606BN was the last SP in the Braniff International Airways dwindling fleet of orange jumbo jets when the airline ceased operations in May 1982. Over-expansion and no clear direction caused the end of a once-great airline. (Robert A. Woodling)

Pan American *Clipper America,* N529PA, was the only SP purchased by Pan Am that was not ordered directly from Boeing. The aircraft is shown with a revised, wider cheatline. (Maurice Bertrand)

A profile shot as United's N150UA. Four of the 11 United SPs would later see service as VIP aircraft, including this example. (Terry Waddington Collection)

A40-SP is one of two SPs in the Sultan of Oman's Royal Flight. (Tommy Mogren Collection)

LN 455/MSN 21933

The livery of CAAC aircraft was dominated by a huge national flag on the tail. B-2444 has been in service since its delivery on June 26, 1980. (ATP/Airliners America)

103

When CAAC was broken up into several regional subsidiaries, Air China received the four SPs, including B-2444. (ATP/Airliners America)

B-2444 was re-registered as B-2438 by Air China on June 3, 1992. (ATP/Airliners America)

LN 467; MSN 21934

The third SP for CAAC was ordered as B-2446 but delivered as N1304E, and became B-2452. (Maurice Bertrand Collection)

CAAC B-2452 was one of four SPs utilized for trans-Pacific flights as well as destinations throughout Asia and Europe. (ATP/Airliners America)

B-2452 shows the Air China livery was basically the same as that flown on CAAC. The fuselage titles were changed and a stylized bird replaced the flag. (Maurice Bertrand Collection)

LN 473/MSN 22302

CAAC 747SP N1301E. Originally ordered by Braniff (as N1608B) and later canceled, the aircraft became the fourth SP delivered to the Chinese airline. The aircraft carried the American registration for almost six years. (The Boeing Company Archives)

105

N1301E was re-registered as B-2454 on January 1, 1989. (Robbie Shaw via Maurice Bertrand)

Air China B-2454 photographed at Zurich in September 1991. (Jean M. Magendie via Jan Mogren Collection)

LN 501/MSN 22483

The first SP for Korean Air Lines, HL7456 is seen on the runway at Paine Field, Everett, Washington. The KAL SPs established nonstop service from New York to Seoul. (The Boeing Company Archives)

A new name and livery for Korean Air Lines. The distinctive sky blue fuselage gives Korean Air 747SP HL7456 a clean, attractive look. (via Eddy Gual)

LN 505/MSN 22495

Qantas VH-EAA takes off from Sydney on its way to California. The SP was an outstanding aircraft for Qantas' routes, able to make nonstop flights across the Pacific. VH-EAA is named *City of Gold Coast-Tweed.* (Julian Green)

Qantas VH-EAA in its beautiful, modern livery. The legendary winged kangaroo is gone from the tail, replaced by a more conventional marsupial. (Maurice Bertrand)

Slight revisions were made to the Qantas tail and titles to provide Australia Asia Airlines VH-EAA its own identity.
(Duncan Stewart via Maurice Bertrand)

LN 507/MSN 22484

HL7457 at Zurich, December 1983. The Korean Air Lines' two SPs were used for the nonstop Seoul-to-New York flights and for service from Seoul to Europe. (J.-F. Boussouge via Jan Mogren Collection)

HL7457 photographed in March 1995. The SPs were configured to carry 12 first-class, 40 business-class and 200 economy-class passengers. (Duncan Stewart via Maurice Bertrand)

LN 529/MSN 22503

HZ-AIF, the first passenger SP for Saudi Arabia, was put into service on nonstop New York–Jeddah and New York–Dhahran routes. (Maurice Bertrand Collection)

LN 534/MSN 22547

China Airlines N4508H coming to a full stop with the thrust-reversers engaged. The placement of the registration numbers high on the tail and on the forward fuselage was very much appreciated by plane spotters. (Maurice Bertrand Collection)

Mandarin Airlines N4508H was removed from service in February 1997 and was prepared for sale in a VIP configuration. (Maurice Bertrand)

LN 537/MSN 22672

A splash of champagne for good luck and Qantas SP VH-EAB *Winton* is christened during a pre-delivery ceremony at the Everett Division plant. Both Qantas SPs were equipped with the option to ferry an extra engine under the port wing. (Museum of Flight Archives)

VH-EAB in the popular "Euro-white" look. The name of the aircraft was changed from *Winton* to *City of Traralgon*. (Jim Thompson)

Australia Asia SP VH-EAB taxies at Sydney airport. Australia Asia used the SPs on the Sydney–Taipei route that parent company Qantas was politically unable to fly. When Qantas privatized, political implications ceased and the aircraft were returned to Qantas colors. (Julian Green)

LN 560/MSN 22750

Saudia HZ-AIJ was built for passenger service and delivered on May 25, 1982. It was transferred from Saudia to the Saudi Royal Flight on October 1, 1992, and re-configured as a VIP aircraft. (Maurice Bertrand collection)

LN 564/MSN 22805

Surviving a nearly disastrous flight from Taipei to Los Angeles in 1985 (see Chapter X), China Airlines N4522V was repaired and returned to regular service. (Brian J. Gore)

A late addition to the Mandarin Airlines fleet, N4522V was leased to the China Airlines subsidiary in February 1997 to replace N4508H. (K. Nakano via Tommy Mogren Collection)

LN 567/MSN 22858

An Iraqi government VIP transport, YI-ALM was photographed in July 1987. The colors are identical to Iraqi Airways, with only the titles differing. The aircraft name *Al-Qadissiya* appears on the forward fuselage. (Tommy Mogren Collection)

A sure target in the Gulf War, YI-ALM was moved for safe keeping to storage in Tunisia, where it remains grounded due to the no-fly restrictions placed on Iraq. (Paul Bannwarth via Jan Mogren Collection)

LN 676/ MSN 23610

Flagship of the United Arab Emirates, the Abu Dhabi aircraft was the last and possibly the most expensive 747SP built. Although A6-ZSN represented the end of SP factory production, its opulence and status have created a demand for many of the existing 747SPs to be retrofitted as VIP aircraft. (Bob Shane)

113

Chapter X
SAFETY

The 747SP has amassed an exceptional safety record in over two decades of service which have included over 2,100,000 flight hours and 385,000 cycles. Not one of the 45 SP airframes has been written off due to accident or mechanical failure. Although several incidents have been reported over the years – with the severity varying from minor to near catastrophic – none have involved the loss of life. Most have involved minor ground collisions or severe clear air turbulence.

The closest a 747SP came to catastrophe was on February 19, 1985. On an otherwise uneventful flight from Taipei, Taiwan, to Los Angeles, China Airlines N4522V (ln 564/msn 22805) lost power in the number four engine. At the time of the incident, the aircraft was over the Pacific Ocean at an altitude of 41,000 feet, approximately 300 miles northeast of San Francisco. During the attempt by the crew to restore normal power to the engine, the aircraft rolled to the right, nosed over, and entered an uncontrolled descent of nearly six miles. The crew was unable to restore the airplane to normal flight until it had descended to 9,500 feet. After regaining control, the captain elected to divert the aircraft to an emergency landing at San Francisco International Airport.

Published reports indicated at 37,000 feet the aircraft's pitch angle was 62 degrees nose-down and it had rolled to 162 degrees. Of the 274 persons aboard, only two received serious injuries and 10 others required minor medical treatment.

The aircraft suffered damage to the left outboard aileron, and the outboard main landing gear doors were ripped away during the descent. About 15 feet of the left stabilizer, including the outboard elevator were torn free, as well as 10 feet of the right stabilizer and half of the elevator. In its report, the National Transportation Safety Board determined that the probable cause of the accident was "the captain's preoccupation with an inflight malfunction and his failure to monitor properly the airplane's flight instruments which resulted in his losing control of the airplane." Also contributing to the accident was "the captain's over-reliance on the autopilot after the loss of thrust on the number four engine." The aircraft was repaired and returned to service with China Airlines.

Damage sustained by the starboard stabilizer during the uncontrolled descent of China Airlines N4522V. The aircraft was recovered and resumed level flight 9,500 feet above the Pacific Ocean. (AP/Wide World Photos)

Chapter XI
THE FUTURE

After two decades of service, the 747SP remains a valuable asset to airlines throughout the world, and will continue to fly passengers well into the next century. As an ever increasing number of SPs are being replaced by even longer range, fuel-efficient Airbus and Boeing aircraft, the role of the aging little 747 as an airliner is shifting from front-line service with the major carriers to the airlines of developing countries. The SP has served with operators from such diverse countries as Kazakhstan, Mauritius, Namibia and Tajikistan.

Many of the SPs leaving airline service are quickly purchased for conversion to government-operated VIP transportation. Currently, twelve 747SP are providing this service for leaders in the Middle East and Asia, with more expected in the future. Having the SPs in VIP service should help to extend their life spans, as they are not flown on a regularly scheduled basis and receive the highest quality maintenance. For example, the SP operated by the government of Abu Dhabi (A6-ZSN, ln 676/msn 23610), has approximately 1,849 hours and 1,328 cycles – the equivalent of approximately 1 hour, 40 minutes per flight – on an airframe that was completed in 1987.

Because of limited use as a VIP aircraft, and the fact that it has been stored in the desert since the beginning of the Gulf War, the Iraqi government SP (YI-ALM, ln 567/msn 22858), which was delivered in 1982, has just 1,970 hours and 688 cycles in its logbook.

Stratospheric Observatory For Infrared Astronomy (SOFIA)

Perhaps the most unusual role yet found for the junior jumbo is the one planned by the National Aeronautics and Space Administration (NASA) for the Stratospheric Observatory For Infrared Astronomy (SOFIA). This airborne observatory will carry astronomers, educators and students to the edges of the stratosphere to peer into the secrets of the universe. The many reasons why the Special Performance 747 was such a revolutionary airliner make it the ideal platform for this new mission: the large fuselage is able to sustain the structural changes necessary to comfortably carry the 98-inch telescope; the SPs ability to maintain altitudes of between 41,000 and 45,000 feet allow it to climb high in the Earth's atmosphere, providing an undistorted view of space; and its speed and range allow it to fly almost anywhere in the world to be positioned for any cosmic occurrence.

On December 16, 1996, NASA awarded an estimated $484.5 million contract to Universities Space Research Association (USRA),

The Stratospheric Observatory For Infrared Astronomy (SOFIA) will become the largest airborne observatory ever built. This specially modified SP (currently N145UA, ln 306/msn 21441) will fly a telescope to altitudes up to nine miles, allowing for clearer images of the universe. (Courtesy of NASA)

to acquire, develop and operate SOFIA. USRA will work with team members Central Texas Airborne Systems, United Airlines, The Astronomical Society of the Pacific, The Seti Institute, Sterling Software, and the University of California at Berkeley and at Los Angeles. The contract has a base period for development plus one five-year operations cycle and an option period for one additional five-year operations cycle. The SOFIA telescope will be provided by the German space agency, Deutsche Agentur für Raumfahrtangelegenheiten (DARA), a partner in the SOFIA project, which is expected to operate for at least 20 years. The contract calls for the selected company to acquire an existing Boeing 747SP aircraft, design and implement a modification program to accommodate installation of a large infrared telescope, test and deliver the flying astronomical observatory to NASA, and provide mission and operations support in five-year increments. The aircraft will operate out of Moffett Federal Airfield, Mountain View, California.

The high altitudes reached by the SP provide a clear, dry environment enabling scientists to study radiant heat patterns from the stars, planets and other celestial sources. Radiation data from astronomical sources cannot typically be collected by sites on the Earth because it is absorbed by atmospheric water vapor before reaching the surface. This applies to most infrared light, gamma rays, x-rays and ultraviolet light. SOFIA overcomes this limitation by operating above more than 85 percent of the Earth's atmosphere and 99 percent of the radiation-absorbing water vapor. SOFIA instruments can be switched, upgraded and be deployed rapidly throughout the northern or southern hemisphere as required. With up to 160 eight-hour flights planned annually, SOFIA will be able to conduct a wide array of scientific investigations and provide educational opportunities for teachers and students.

The SOFIA concept is an updated version of its predecessor, the Kuiper Airborne Observatory (KAO), named for Gerald P. Kuiper, a University of Arizona astronomer who conceived the idea of a flying astronomical observatory in the mid-1960s. KAO was a converted Lockheed C-141 transport equipped with a 36-inch reflecting infrared telescope. It began in 1974 and conducted important scientific missions for over 22 years. KAO's accomplishments include the first sighting of the rings of Uranus and the identification of Pluto's atmosphere. SOFIA's telescope will be more than 2.5 times larger than KAO's, affording even greater opportunity for scientific discovery.

The dedication of SOFIA took place in the United Airlines' maintenance base at San Francisco International Airport on April 11, 1997. The acquired aircraft, N145UA (ln 306/msn 21441), was the only SP in United's fleet painted in the gray and blue livery. It was retired from service on October 20, 1994, and stored in the dry atmosphere of the Las Vegas desert until February 17, 1997, then ferried to San Francisco. New titles were applied to the United colors, and a rectangle of black paint was applied where the opening for the telescope will be installed. United Airlines, part of the contract winning team, will provide flight crews for the SOFIA

A close-up look at SOFIA N145UA on the ramp at the United Airlines Maintenance facility in San Francisco. Note SP titles under the nose. (Ed Davies)

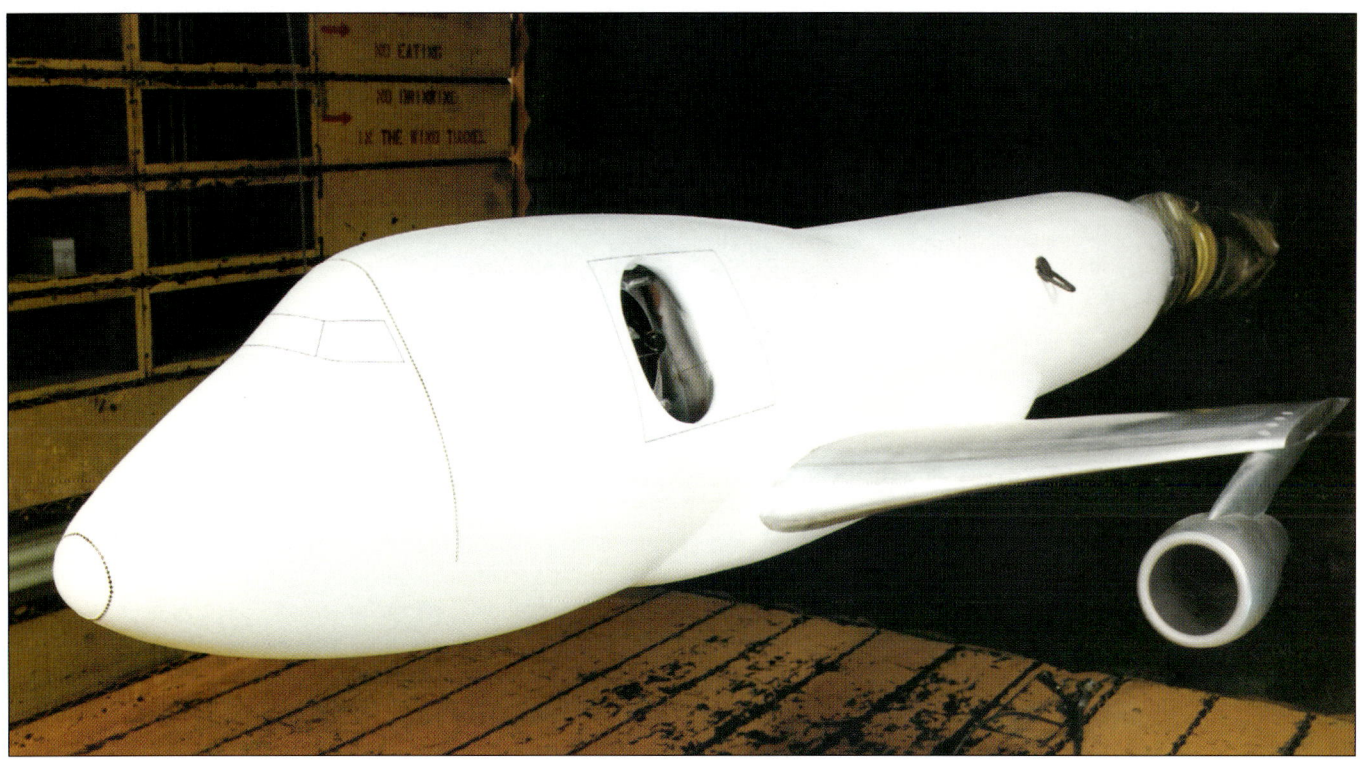

Early in the project, wind tunnel testing was completed at NASA Ames Research Center to determine the optimum location for placement of the telescope. (NASA Photo via Ron Strong)

flights through its UAL Services Division, and the aircraft will be maintained at United's San Francisco maintenance base. Following dedication ceremonies, the aircraft was again ferried, this time to Waco, Texas, where Raytheon E-Systems' Airborne Systems Division will instrument the aircraft to obtain readings during tests. The information from these tests will be used to develop plans to modify the SP to accommodate the telescope, which will be housed in an unpressurized structure in the aft fuselage, forward of the rear pressure bulkhead. Raytheon is designing a new pressure bulkhead that will be situated just aft of the trailing edge of the wing. Before a mission, the telescope and its housing will be artificially cooled to match the air temperature at altitude before the observation door is opened, to prevent fogging. Wind tunnel tests will determine the optimal arrangement for the door. The first design caused unsatisfactory drag, which is largely avoided by a new arrangement which allows the door to move inside the cabin for storage. The revision would require that a raised area be installed on the side of the fuselage to accommodate the door. Full conversion work is scheduled to begin in the fall of 1998, with the first missions taking place in late 2001.

Appendix I
INDIVIDUAL AIRCRAFT DISPOSITION

This table, compiled largely from the Airclaims Client Aviation System Enquiry (CASE) database provides the most significant information on the operational history of each of the 45 Boeing 747SP aircraft, organized in order of actual production by the line number (LN). Since the SP was considered a variation of the 747 and not a separate type, it does not have its own specific range of line numbers (for example, ln 281 was a 747-136, ln 282 a 747SP-44, and ln 283 a 747-212B). The manufacturer's serial number (MSN), identifies the airframe for legal purposes and remains constant throughout its life. The third column has two entries for each airplane: The first line is the aircraft series (Series), a numeric or alpha-numeric suffix issued by Boeing to identify the aircraft by customer. Below the series number is the block number (Block). This is an alpha-numeric designation used internally by Boeing. The alpha characters in the SP's block number were determined by the engine type; RG = Pratt and Whitney JT9D-7, RH = Rolls Royce RB.211-524.

Column four (Registration Number) provides a complete history of the aircraft by its official registration. In addition to airline and government registrations, Boeing test registrations (when reported) are also included. Boeing is issued "fly-away" registration numbers by the Federal Aviation Administration. These numbers are not necessarily specific to any one aircraft, and may be used repeatedly. The operator of the aircraft (Aircraft Operator) is shown by name. Due to space limitations, this column lists only the actual operator of the aircraft, rather than the airline, bank or finance company which legally owned the aircraft. The next two columns (Event Date and Event Description) note major events in the history of each aircraft including when it was originally ordered, rolled out, its first flight, delivery, and transfer to new owners or leasees. The status of each aircraft as of publication is also listed. There is no specific date listed for the break up of the first five SPs. Immediately after arrival, valuable equipment, such as engines, were removed at Ardmore, Oklahoma, and returned to United Airlines. All other usable parts were subsequently taken off the aircraft. All dates are listed in the American format of month-day-year. The final two columns list the actual flight hours (Total Hours) and the number of takeoffs and landings (Total Cycles) for each aircraft as reported to The Boeing Company. If an aircraft is listed as "broken up," the hours and cycles listed represent the final totals. Total hours and cycles are current as of February 1997.

Abbreviations used in table: ADM = Ardmore, Oklahoma; MZJ = Marana, Arizona; not op = not operated; TOE = Tozeur, Tunisia; WFU = Withdrawn From Use.

LN	MSN	Series/Block	Registration Number	Aircraft Operator	Event Date	Event Description	Total Hours	Total Cycles
265	21022	SP-21	N530PA	Pan American	09-10-73	Ordered		
		RG001	N530PA	Boeing	05-19-75	New aircraft rolled out		
			N747SP	Boeing	07-04-75	New aircraft first flight		
			N530PA	Pan American	04-26-76	New aircraft delivered		
			N140UA	United Airlines	02-11-86	Leased		
			N140UA	United Airlines	11-94	WFU - parked		
			N140UA	United Airlines	11-05-95	Final flight		
						Broken up - ADM	78,312	10,700
268	21023	SP-21	N531PA	Pan American	09-10-73	Ordered		
		RG002	N247SP	Boeing	06-30-75	New aircraft rolled out		
			N247SP	Boeing	08-14-75	New aircraft first flight		
			N531PA	Pan American	05-12-76	New aircraft delivered		
			N141UA	United Airlines	02-11-86	Leased		
			N141UA	United Airlines	07-94	WFU - parked		
			N141UA	United Airlines	07-13-95	Final flight		
						Broken up - ADM	78,442	10,366
270	21024	SP-21	N532PA	Pan American	09-10-73	Ordered		
		RG003	N347SP	Boeing	09-03-75	New aircraft rolled out		
			N347SP	Boeing	10-10-75	New aircraft first flight		
			N532PA	Pan American	03-29-76	New aircraft delivered		
			N142UA	United Airlines	02-11-86	Leased		
			N142UA	United Airlines	07-94	WFU - parked		
			N142UA	United Airlines	11-04-95	Final flight		
						Broken up - ADM	79,412	10,590

LN	MSN	Series/Block	Registration Number	Aircraft Operator	Event Date	Event Description	Total Hours	Total Cycles
273	21025	SP-21 RG004	N533PA N40135 N40135 N533PA N143UA N143UA N143UA N143UA N143UA	Pan American Boeing Boeing Pan American United Airlines United Airlines United Airlines United Airlines United Airlines	09-10-73 10-08-75 11-03-75 03-05-76 02-11-86 10-03-93 04-94 10-94 07-14-95	Ordered New aircraft rolled out New aircraft first flight New aircraft delivered Leased WFU - parked Returned to operation WFU - parked Final flight Broken up - ADM	78,941	10,733
275	20998	SP-86 RG101	EP-IAA EP-IAA EP-IAA EP-IAA EP-IAA	Iran Air Boeing Boeing Iran Air Iran Air	10-10-73 11-11-75 02-20-76 03-12-76	Ordered New aircraft rolled out New aircraft first flight New aircraft delivered Operational	15,776	4,684
278	20999	SP-86 RG102	EP-IAB EP-IAB EP-IAB EP-IAB EP-IAB	Iran Air Boeing Boeing Iran Air Iran Air	10-10-73 12-16-75 04-22-76 05-10-76	Ordered New aircraft rolled out New aircraft first flight New aircraft delivered Operational	15,979	4,576
280	21132	SP-44 RG121	ZS-SPA ZS-SPA ZS-SPA ZS-SPA ZS-SPA ZS-SPA 3B-NAJ ZS-SPA ZS-SPA ZS-SPA	South African Boeing Boeing South African Luxair South African Air Mauritius South African Alliance Alliance	07-16-74 01-27-76 02-17-76 03-23-76 10-80 01-81 04-01-87 05-31-94 02-95	Ordered New aircraft rolled out New aircraft first flight New aircraft delivered Leased - (not op) Returned Leased Returned off lease Wet-leased Operational	60,873	12,482
282	21133	SP-44 RG122	ZS-SPB ZS-SPB ZS-SPB ZS-SPB 7Q-YKL ZS-SPB LX-LGX ZS-SPB ZS-SPB ZS-SPB ZS-SPB ZS-SPB ZS-SPB ZS-SPB ZS-SPB ZS-SPB	South African Boeing Boeing South African Air Malawi South African Luxair South African Flitestar (Trek) Flitestar (Trek) South African Panair (not op) Cameroon Airlines Panair (not op) Air Namibia Air Namibia	07-16-74 02-24-76 03-10-76 04-23-76 04-12-85 05-11-85 11-01-87 09-02-93 09-03-93 04-11-94 04-11-94 10-95 04-96 05-96 06-96	Ordered New aircraft rolled out New aircraft first flight New aircraft delivered Leased Returned Wet-leased Returned - not op Wet-leased Operator ceased ops Returned Purchased Leased Returned Leased Operational	54,486	11,045
284	21174	SP-94 RG141	YK-AHA YK-AHA YK-AHA YK-AHA YK-AHA	Syrianair Boeing Boeing Syrianair Syrianair	12-06-74 03-23-76 04-15-76 05-21-76	Ordered New aircraft rolled out New aircraft first flight New aircraft delivered Operational	19,951	8,609

LN	MSN	Series/Block	Registration Number	Aircraft Operator	Event Date	Event Description	Total Hours	Total Cycles
286	21026	SP-21 RG005	N534PA	Pan American	09-10-73	Ordered		
			N534PA	Boeing	04-19-76	New aircraft rolled out		
			N534PA	Boeing	05-07-76	New aircraft first flight		
			N534PA	Pan American	05-28-76	New aircraft delivered		
			N144UA	United Airlines	02-11-86	Leased		
			N144UA	United Airlines	02-94	WFU - parked		
			N144UA	United Airlines	04-94	Returned to operation		
			N144UA	United Airlines	07-12-94	WFU - parked		
			N144UA	United Airlines	03-07-96	Final flight		
						Broken up - ADM	78,870	10,530
288	21134	SP-44 RG123	ZS-SPC	South African	07-16-74	Ordered		
			N8297V	Boeing	05-17-76	New aircraft rolled out		
			N8297V	Boeing	06-04-76	New aircraft first flight		
			ZS-SPC	South African	06-17-76	New aircraft delivered		
			3B-NAG	Air Mauritius	10-28-84	Leased		
			ZS-SPC	South African	11-10-94	Returned		
			ZS-SPC	Avia (not op)	03-95	Leased		
			ZS-SPC	Avia	04-24-95	Returned to operation		
			ZS-SPC	Avia	08-02-95	Operator ceased service		
			ZS-SPC	South African	08-02-95	Returned		
			ZS-SPC	Air Namibia	10-95	Leased		
			ZS-SPC	South African	06-96	Returned		
			ZS-SPC	South African		Operational	60,237	12,257
290	21175	SP-94 RG142	YK-AHB	Syrianair	12-06-74	Ordered		
			YK-AHB	Boeing	06-15-76	New aircraft rolled out		
			YK-AHB	Boeing	07-01-76	New aircraft first flight		
			YK-AHB	Syrianair	07-16-76	New aircraft delivered		
			YK-AHB	Syrianair		Operational	20,476	8,821
293	21253	SP-44 RG124	ZS-SPD	South African	08-28-75	Ordered		
			ZS-SPD	Boeing	07-28-76	New aircraft rolled out		
			ZS-SPD	Boeing	08-27-76	New aircraft first flight		
			ZS-SPD	South African	09-10-76	New aircraft delivered		
			CN-RMS	Royal Air Maroc	03-15-85	Leased		
			CN-RMS	Royal Air Maroc	09-04-86	Purchased		
			LX-ACO	Corsair	10-13-94	Purchased		
			F-GTOM	Corsair	03-29-96	Re-registered		
			F-GTOM	Corsair		Operational	55,851	11,862
298	21254	SP-44 RG125	ZS-SPE	South African	08-28-75	Ordered		
			ZS-SPE	Boeing	10-21-76	New aircraft rolled out		
			ZS-SPE	Boeing	05-11-76	New aircraft first flight		
			ZS-SPE	South African	11-22-76	New aircraft delivered		
			3B-NAR	Air Mauritius	11-01-91	Leased		
			ZS-SPE	South African	06-15-92	Returned		
			V5-SPE	Air Namibia	03-25-93	Leased		
			ZS-SPE	South African	05-12-93	Returned		
			ZS-SPE	South African		Operational	57,346	11,786
301	21263	SP-44 RG126	ZS-SPF	South African	10-27-75	Ordered		
			ZS-SPF	Boeing	12-22-76	New aircraft rolled out		
			ZS-SPF	Boeing	01-14-77	New aircraft first flight		
			ZS-SPF	South African	01-31-77	New aircraft delivered		
			LX-LTM	Luxair	10-80	Leased (not op)		
			ZS-SPF	South African	12-80	Returned		
			3B-NAO	Air Mauritius	09-30-88	Leased		
			ZS-SPF	South African	01-89	Returned		
			LXLGY	Luxair	08-01-89	Leased (not op)		
			LX-LGY	UTA	08-01-89	Sub-leased		
			ZS-SPF	South African	11-01-89	Returned		
			V5-SPF	Namib Air	04-01-90	Leased		
			V5-SPF	Air Namiba	10-15-91	New name		
			V5-SPF	Air Namibia		Operational	56,236	12,028

LN	MSN	Series/Block	Registration Number	Aircraft Operator	Event Date	Event Description	Total Hours	Total Cycles
304	21300	SP-09 RG171	B-1862 N8290V N8290V B-1862 B-1862 B-1862	China Airlines Boeing Boeing China Airlines Mandarin Airlines Mandarin Airlines	02-03-76 02-28-77 03-18-77 04-06-77 03-01-93	Ordered New aircraft rolled out New aircraft first flight New aircraft delivered Leased Operational	70,581	15,175
306	21441	SP-21 RG091	N536PA N536PA N536PA N536PA N145UA N145UA N145UA N145UA N145UA N145UA	Pan American Boeing Boeing Pan American United Airlines United Airlines United Airlines United Airlines NASA NASA	12-09-76 04-07-77 04-25-77 05-06-77 02-11-86 09-20-93 04-94 10-20-94 03-97	Ordered New aircraft rolled out New aircraft first flight New aircraft delivered Purchased WFU - parked Returned to operation WFU - parked Purchased NASA/SOFIA Undergoing conversion	74,526	10,114
307	21093	SP-86 RG103	EP-IAC EP-IAC EP-IAC EP-IAC EP-IAC	Iran Air Boeing Boeing Iran Air Iran Air	06-18-74 04-27-77 05-16-77 05-27-77	Ordered New aircraft rolled out New aircraft first flight New aircraft delivered Operational	12,140	3,597
325	21547	SP-21 RG006	N537PA N537PA N537PA N537PA N146UA N146UA N146UA N146UA	Pan American Boeing Boeing Pan American United Airlines United Airlines United Airlines United Airlines	07-09-77 04-20-78 05-05-78 06-09-78 02-11-86 05-17-94 05-24-95	Ordered New aircraft rolled out New aircraft first flight New aircraft delivered Leased WFU - parked Ferry flight; stored - MZJ For sale	70,184	9,220
329	21652	SP-68 RH101	HZ-HM1 N1780B N1780B HZ-HM1 HZ-HM1B HZ-HM1B	Govt. of Saudi Arabia Boeing Boeing Govt. of Saudi Arabia Govt. of Saudi Arabia Govt. of Saudi Arabia	11-09-77 05-24-78 08-28-78 07-11-79 09-30-84	Ordered New aircraft rolled out New aircraft first flight New aircraft delivered Re-registered Operational	3,465	2,019
331	21548	SP-21 RG007	N538PA N538PA N538PA N538PA N147UA N147UA N147UA N147UA	Pan American Boeing Boeing Pan American United Airlines United Airlines United Airlines United Airlines	07-09-77 06-12-78 06-30-78 07-12-78 02-11-86 10-12-94 11-30-95	Ordered New aircraft rolled out New aircraft first flight New aircraft delivered Leased WFU - parked Ferry flight; stored - MZJ For sale	71,470	9,197
367	21648	SP-21 RG008	N539PA N539PA N539PA N539PA N148UA N148UA VR-BAT VP-BAT VP-BAT	Pan American Boeing Boeing Pan American United Airlines United Airlines Govt. of Qatar Govt. of Qatar Govt. of Qatar	12-15-77 03-09-79 03-30-79 04-20-79 02-11-86 04-24-94 11-20-95 07-01-97	Ordered New aircraft rolled out New aircraft first flight New aircraft delivered Purchased WFU - parked Leased Re-registered Operational	65,154	8,507

LN	MSN	Series/Block	Registration Number	Aircraft Operator	Event Date	Event Description	Total Hours	Total Cycles
371	21758	SP-86 RG104	EP-IAD N1800B N1800B EP-IAD EP-IAD	Iran Air Boeing Boeing Iran Air Iran Air	06-01-78 04-02-79 04-26-79 07-12-79	Ordered New aircraft rolled out New aircraft first flight New aircraft delivered Operational	5,763	2,230
373	21649	SP-21 RG009	N540PA N540PA N540PA N540PA N149UA N149UA N149UA N149UA N149UA V8-JBB V8-JP1 V8-AC1 V8-AC1 V8-AC1	Pan American Boeing Boeing Pan American United Airlines United Airlines Tajik Air United Airlines United Airlines Govt. of Brunei Govt. of Brunei Govt. of Brunei Govt. of Brunei Govt. of Brunei	12-15-77 04-12-79 05-01-79 05-11-79 02-11-86 10-02-93 11-28-93 02-14-94 03-07-94 08-95 03-96 04-96 12-96	Ordered New aircraft rolled out New aircraft first flight New aircraft delivered Purchased WFU - parked Leased Repossessed Ferry flight; stored Purchased (not op) Re-registered (not op) Re-registered (not op) Returned to operation Operational	65,452	8,500
405	21785	SP-27 RG161	N603BN N603BN N603BN N603BN N603BN N351AS A40-SO A40-SO A40-SO	Braniff Boeing Boeing Braniff Boeing (not op) Boeing (not op) Govt. of Oman Govt. of Oman Govt. of Oman	05-22-78 09-18-79 10-07-79 10-30-79 01-23-81 08-81 07-02-84 07-87	Ordered New aircraft rolled out New aircraft first flight New aircraft delivered Purchased Re-registered Purchased (not op) Returned to operation Operational	7,510	1,763
413	21786	SP-27 RG162	N604BN N604BN N604BN N604BN LV-OHV 3B-NAQ A7-ABM A7-ABM A7-AHM A7-AHM A7-AHM	Braniff Boeing Boeing Braniff Aer. Argentinas Air Mauritius Qatar Airways Govt. of Qatar Govt. of Qatar Govt. of Qatar Govt. of Qatar	05-22-78 10-22-79 11-29-79 04-23-80 09-12-80 05-31-90 02-08-96 07-96 11-96 11-96	Ordered New aircraft rolled out New aircraft first flight New aircraft delivered Purchased Purchased Purchased Purchased Re-registered Parked - VIP Conversion Operational	51,288	9,299
415	21961	SP-31 RG191	N58201 N58201 N58201 N58201 A6-SMR A6-SMR	Trans World Boeing Boeing Trans World Govt. of Dubai Govt. of Dubai	10-17-78 10-30-79 12-02-79 04-14-80 02-22-85	Ordered New aircraft rolled out New aircraft first flight New aircraft delivered Purchased Operational	20,967	4,882
433	21932	SP-J6 RG211	B-2442 B-2442 B-2442 B-2442 B-2442 B-2442	CAAC Boeing Boeing CAAC Air China Air China	12-19-78 01-24-80 02-14-80 02-26-80 07-01-88	Ordered New aircraft rolled out New aircraft first flight New aircraft delivered Transferred Operational	48,119	12,334

LN	MSN	Series/Block	Registration Number	Aircraft Operator	Event Date	Event Description	Total Hours	Total Cycles
439	21962	SP-31 RG192	N57202 N57202 N57202 N57202 N57202 N57202 N57202 N57202 N57202 N601AA N601AA N601AA UN-001 P4-AFE P4-AFE	Trans World Boeing Boeing Trans World Boeing Trans World Jet Aviation Jet Associates Intl. American American American American Kazakhstan Airlines Govt. of Brunei Govt. of Brunei	10-17-78 02-19-80 03-12-80 03-21-80 02-01-81 06-01-81 07-24-84 12-85 07-16-86 12-86 05-22-87 07-18-92 01-06-94 03-96 	Ordered New aircraft rolled out New aircraft first flight New aircraft delivered Leased Returned Purchased (not op) Purchased (not op) Purchased (not op) Re-registered (not op) Returned to operation WFU - parked Purchased Leased Operational		
							32,695	4,760
441	21963	SP-31 RG193	N57203 N57203 N57203 N57203 N57203 N602AA N602AA N602AA N602AA A6-SMM A6-SMM	Trans World Boeing Boeing Trans World American American American American Govt. of Dubai Govt. of Dubai Govt. of Dubai	10-17-78 02-27-80 04-11-80 05-08-80 10-16-86 01-87 05-21-87 07-20-92 04-07-94 02-17-95 	Ordered New aircraft rolled out New aircraft first flight New aircraft delivered Purchased (not op) Re-registered (not op) Returned to operation WFU - parked Purchased (not op) Returned to operation Operational		
							43,646	6,671
445	22298	SP-09 RG172	B-1861 B-1880 B-1880 B-1880 B-1880 B-1880	China Airlines Boeing Boeing China Airlines Mandarin Airlines Mandarin Airlines	12-08-78 03-16-80 04-18-80 04-30-80 08-15-92 	Ordered New aircraft rolled out New aircraft first flight New aircraft delivered Leased Operational		
							63,601	12,215
447	21992	SP-27 RG163	N606BN N606BN N606BN N606BN N606BN N529PA N150UA N150UA N150UA A40-SP A40-SP	Braniff Boeing Boeing Braniff Braniff Pan American United Airlines United Airlines Govt. of Oman Govt. of Oman Govt. of Oman	12-18-78 03-24-80 05-19-80 05-30-80 05-13-82 09-23-83 02-11-86 05-31-92 08-21-92 04-29-93 	Ordered New aircraft rolled out New aircraft first flight New aircraft delivered Ceased operations Purchased Purchased WFU - parked Purchased (not op) Returned to operation Operational		
							43,898	6,671
455	21933	SP-J6 RG212	B-2444 B-2444 B-2444 B-2444 B-2444 B-2438 B-2438	CAAC Boeing Boeing CAAC Air China Air China Air China	12-19-78 04-25-80 06-06-80 06-26-80 07-01-88 06-03-92 	Ordered New aircraft rolled out New aircraft first flight New aircraft delivered Transferred Re-Registered Operational		
							43,809	10,952
467	21934	SP-J6 RG213	B-2446 N1304E N1304E N1304E B-2452 B-2452 B-2452	CAAC Boeing Boeing CAAC CAAC Air China Air China	12-19-78 06-17-80 07-11-80 09-23-80 01-01-88 07-01-88 	Ordered New aircraft rolled out New aircraft first flight New aircraft delivered Re-Registered Transferred Operational		
							49,732	11,520

123

LN	MSN	Series/Block	Registration Number	Aircraft Operator	Event Date	Event Description	Total Hours	Total Cycles
473	22302	SP-27 RG164	N1608B N1608B N1608B N1608B B-2454 N1301E N1301E B-2454 B-2454	Braniff Boeing Boeing Braniff CAAC CAAC Air China Air China Air China	07-24-79 07-14-80 12-02-80 05-13-82 12-23-82 06-15-83 07-01-88 01-01-89 	Ordered New aircraft rolled out New aircraft first flight Order cancelled Ordered New aircraft delivered Transferred Re-registered Operational	43,022	10,430
501	22483	SP-B5 RG221	HL7456 HL7456 HL7456 HL7456 HL7456	Korean Air Lines Boeing Boeing Korean Air Lines Korean Air	04-10-79 11-24-80 12-23-80 01-22-81 	Ordered New aircraft rolled out New aircraft first flight New aircraft delivered Operational	63,433	8,564
505	22495	SP-38 RH111	VH-EAA VH-EAA VH-EAA VH-EAA VH-EAA VH-EAA VH-EAA	Qantas Boeing Boeing Qantas Australia Asia Qantas Qantas	01-16-80 12-18-80 01-11-81 01-19-81 03-25-94 06-27-96 	Ordered New aircraft rolled out New aircraft first flight New aircraft delivered Transferred Transferred Operational	53,509	9,396
507	22484	SP-B5 RG222	HL7457 HL7457 HL7457 HL7457 HL7457	Korean Air Lines Boeing Boeing Korean Air Lines Korean Air	04-10-79 01-09-81 01-30-81 03-18-81 	Ordered New aircraft rolled out New aircraft first flight New aircraft delivered Operational	62,386	8,380
529	22503	SP-68 RH121	HZ-AIF HZ-AIF HZ-AIF HZ-AIF HZ-AIF	Saudia Boeing Boeing Saudia Saudia	12-19-79 05-13-81 06-04-81 06-23-81 	Ordered New aircraft rolled out New aircraft first flight New aircraft delivered Operational	32,137	8,491
534	22547	SP-09 RG173	B-1882 N1785B N1785B N4508H N4508H N4508H N4508H	China Airlines Boeing Boeing China Airlines Mandarin Airlines China Airlines 	03-80 06-23-81 07-20-81 09-30-81 10-01-91 02-97 	Ordered New aircraft rolled out New aircraft first flight New aircraft delivered Wet-leased Returned Sold - VIP conversion	58,834	10,547
537	22672	SP-38 RH112	VH-EAB N1791B N1791B VH-EAB VH-EAB VH-EAB VH-EAB	Qantas Boeing Boeing Qantas Australia Asia Qantas Qantas	06-80 07-20-81 08-03-81 08-31-81 04-18-94 06-27-96 	Ordered New aircraft rolled out New aircraft first flight New aircraft delivered Transferred Transferred Operational	47,600	10,385
560	22750	SP-68 RH122	HZ-AIJ N6046P N6046P HZ-AIJ HZ-AIJ HZ-AIJ	Saudia Boeing Boeing Saudia Govt. of Saudi Arabia Govt. of Saudi Arabia	03-81 03-29-82 04-13-82 05-25-82 10-01-92 	Ordered New aircraft rolled out New aircraft first flight New aircraft delivered Transferred Operational	20,864	4,351

LN	MSN	Series/Block	Registration Number	Aircraft Operator	Event Date	Event Description	Total Hours	Total Cycles
564	22805	SP-09 RG174	N4522V N4522V N4522V N4522V N4522V N4522V	China Airlines Boeing Boeing China Airlines Mandarin Airlines Mandarin Airlines	05-81 05-24-82 06-10-82 06-29-82 02-97	Ordered New aircraft rolled out New aircraft first flight New aircraft delivered Wet-leased Operational	54,850	10,751
567	22858	SP-70 RG095	YI-ALM YI-ALM YI-ALM YI-ALM YI-ALM YI-ALM	Iraqi Airways Boeing Boeing Iraqi Airways Govt. of Iraq Govt. of Iraq	1981 07-07-82 08-02-82 08-30-82 08-30-82 01-16-91	Ordered New aircraft rolled out New aircraft first flight New aircraft delivered Transferred WFU - parked - TOE	1,970	688
676	23610	SP-Z5 RH102	A6-ZSN N60659 N60659 N60697 A6-ZSN A6-ZSN	Govt. of Abu Dhabi Boeing Boeing Govt. of Abu Dhabi Govt. of Abu Dhabi Govt. of Abu Dhabi	06-86 03-13-87 03-31-87 12-09-89 12-89	Ordered New aircraft rolled out New aircraft first flight New aircraft delivered Re-registered Operational	1,849	1,328

Saudia SP with Boeing registration N6046P (ln 560/msn 22750). The aircraft was re-registered HZ-AIJ prior to delivery. (The Boeing Company Archives)

Appendix II
AIRCRAFT NAMES

This listing of names assigned by airlines and governments to their 747SP aircraft is as complete and accurate as possible. If more than one name exists for a single aircraft, it is listed chronologically. Since airliner names are often exchanged or applied on a temporary basis, dates of changes are not furnished as airline records tend to be incomplete.

LN	MSN	REGISTRATION	OPERATOR	NAME
265	21022	N530PA	Pan American	Clipper Mayflower
268	21023	N531PA	Pan American	Clipper Liberty Bell
				Clipper Freedom
270	21024	N532PA	Pan American	Clipper Constitution
273	21025	N533PA	Pan American	Clipper Freedom
				Clipper Liberty Bell
				Clipper New Horizons
				Clipper Young America
				Clipper San Francisco
				Clipper New Horizons
				Clipper Young America
275	20998	EP-IAA	Iran Air	Fars
				Kurdistan
278	20999	EP-IAB	Iran Air	Kurdistan
				Khorasan
280	21132	ZS-SPA	South African	Matroosberg
		3B-NAJ	Air Mauritius	Chateau Mon Plaisir
282	21133	ZS-SPB	South African	Outeniqua
		7Q-YKL	Air Malawi	Mulanje
		ZS-SPB	Trek Airways	Luxavia Star
284	21174	YK-AHA	Syrianair	November 16
286	21026	N534PA	Pan American	Clipper Great Republic
288	21134	ZS-SPC	South African	Maluti
		3B-NAG	Air Mauritius	Chateau de Reduit
		ZS-SPC	AVIA	Gauteng
290	21175	YK-AHB	Syrianair	Arab Solidarity
293	21253	ZS-SPD	South African	Majuba
298	21254	ZS-SPE	South African	Hantam
		3B-NAR	Air Mauritius	Chateau Labourdonnais
301	21263	ZS-SPF	South African	Soutpansberg
		V5-SPF	Namib Air/Air Namibia	Etosha
306	21441	N536PA	Pan American	Clipper Lindbergh
307	21093	EP-IAC	Iran Air	Khuzestan
				Fars
325	21547	N537PA	Pan American	Clipper High Flyer
				Clipper Washington
331	21548	N538PA	Pan American	Clipper Fleetwing
				Clipper Plymouth Rock
				Clipper Fleetwing
				Clipper Princess Grace
367	21648	N539PA	Pan American	Clipper Black Hawk
				Clipper Liberty Bell
373	21649	N540PA	Pan American	Clipper White Falcon
				Clipper Flying Arrow
				Clipper Star of the Union
				China Clipper
		N149UA	Tajik Air	Snow Leopard
413	21786	3B-NAQ	Air Mauritius	Chateau Benares
439	21962	UN-001	Kazakhstan Airlines	Sunkar
447	21992	N529PA	Pan American	Clipper America
505	22495	VH-EAA	Qantas	City of Gold Coast-Tweed
			Australia Asia	City of Gold Coast-Tweed
537	22672	VH-EAB	Qantas	Winton
			Qantas	City of Traralgon
			Australia Asia	City of Traralgon
567	22858	YI-ALM	Iraq Government	Al-Qadissiya

Appendix III
REGISTRATION INDEX

Registration	LN	MSN
UNITED ARAB EMIRATES		
A6-SMM	441	21963
A6-SMR	415	21961
A6-ZSN	676	23610
QATAR		
A7-ABM	413	21786
A7-AHM	413	21786
OMAN		
A40-SO	405	21785
A40-SP	447	21992
CHINA		
B-1861	445	22298
B-1862	304	21300
B-1880	445	22298
B-1882	534	22547
B-2438	455	21933
B-2442	433	21932
B-2444	455	21933
B-2446	467	21934
B-2452	467	21934
B-2454	473	22302
MOROCCO		
CN-RMS	293	21253
IRAN		
EP-IAA	275	20998
EP-IAB	278	20999
EP-IAC	307	21093
EP-IAD	371	21758
FRANCE		
F-GTOM	293	21253
SOUTH KOREA		
HL-7456	501	22483
HL-7457	507	22484
SAUDI ARABIA		
HZ-AIF	529	22503
HZ-AIJ	560	22750
HZ-HM1	329	21652
HZ-HM1B	329	21652
ARGENTINA		
LV-OHV	413	21786
LUXEMBOURG		
LX-ACO	293	21253
LX-LGX	282	21133
LX-LGY	301	21263
LX-LTM	301	21263

Registration	LN	MSN
UNITED STATES OF AMERICA		
N140UA	265	21022
N141UA	268	21023
N142UA	270	21024
N143UA	273	21025
N144UA	286	21026
N145UA	306	21441
N146UA	325	21547
N147UA	331	21548
N148UA	367	21648
N149UA	373	21649
N150UA	447	21992
N247SP	268	21023
N347SP	270	21024
N351AS	405	21785
N529PA	447	21992
N530PA	265	21022
N531PA	268	21023
N532PA	270	21024
N533PA	273	21025
N534PA	286	21026
N536PA	306	21441
N537PA	325	21547
N538PA	331	21548
N539PA	367	21648
N540PA	373	21649
N601AA	439	21962
N602AA	441	21963
N603BN	405	21785
N604BN	413	21786
N606BN	447	21992
N747SP	265	21022
N1301E	473	22302
N1304E	467	21934
N1608B	473	22302
N1780B	329	21652
N1785B	534	22547
N1791B	537	22672
N1800B	371	21758
N4508H	534	22547
N4522V	564	22805
N6046P	560	22750
N8290V	304	21300
N8297V	288	21134
N40135	273	21025
N57202	439	21962
N57203	441	21963
N58201	415	21961
N60659	676	23610
N60697	676	23610

Registration	LN	MSN
ARUBA		
P4-AFE	439	21962
KAZAKHSTAN		
UN-001	439	21962
AUSTRALIA		
VH-EAA	505	22495
VH-EAB	537	22672
BERMUDA		
VP-BAT	367	21648
VR-BAT	367	21648
NAMIBIA		
V5-SPE	298	21254
V5-SPF	301	21263
BRUNEI		
V8-AC1	373	21649
V8-JBB	373	21649
V8-JP1	373	21649
IRAQ		
YI-ALM	567	22858
SYRIA		
YK-AHA	284	21174
YK-AHB	290	21175
SOUTH AFRICA		
ZS-SPA	280	21132
ZS-SPB	282	21133
ZS-SPC	288	21134
ZS-SPD	293	21253
ZS-SPE	298	21254
ZS-SPF	301	21263
MAURITIUS		
3B-NAG	288	21134
3B-NAJ	280	21132
3B-NAO	301	21263
3B-NAQ	413	21786
3B-NAR	298	21254
MALAWI		
7Q-YKL	282	21133

Appendix IV
BIBLIOGRAPHY

Books
Bauer, Eugene E. *Contrails: A Boeing Salesman Reminisces*. Enumclaw, Wa.: TABA Publishing, Inc. 1996. ISBN 1-879242-07-9
Bowers, Peter M. *Boeing Aircraft Since 1916*. London: Putnam Books, 1989. ISBN 0-85177-804-6
Davies, R.E.G. *Pan Am: An Airline and its Aircraft*. New York: Orion Books, 1987. ISBN 0-517-56639-7
—. *Saudia: An Airline and its Aircraft*. McLean, Va.: Paladwr Press, 1995. ISBN 0-962-6483-7-X
Eastwood, A.B. & Roach, J.R. *Jet Airliner Production List, Vol. 1*. Middlesex, UK: The Aviation Hobby Shop, 1995. ISBN 0-907178-54-5
Falconer, Jonathan. *Boeing 747 in Colour*. Shepperton, UK: Ian Allen Ltd., 1993. ISBN 0-7110-2188-0
Gilchrist, Peter. *Modern Civil Aircraft, Vol 4, Boeing 747*. Shepperton, UK: Ian Allen Ltd., 1992. ISBN 0-7110-2050-7
Glines, Carroll V. *Round-The-World Flights*, 2nd Edition. Blue Ridge Summit, Pa; TAB Aero, 1992. ISBN 0-8306-3393-6
Klee, Ulrich. *JP Airline-Fleets* (various issues). Glattbrugg, Switzerland: Bucher & Co.
Lester, Valerie. *Fasten Your Seat Belts!, History and Heroism in the Pan Am Cabin*. McLean, Va.: Paladwr Press, 1995. ISBN 0-9626483-8-8
Lucas, Jim. *Boeing 747: The First Twenty Years*. London: Browcom Group, 1988. ISBN 0-946141-37-1
Shaw, Robbie. *Boeing 747*. London: Osprey Publishing, 1994. ISBN 1-85532-420-2
Tomkins, B. *World Airline Colour Schemes, Vol. One*. Hounslow, UK: Airline Publications & Sales Ltd. 1977
Waddington, Terry. *Great Airliners Series, Vol. Two, Douglas DC-8*. Miami, Fl.: World Transport Press, 1996. ISBN 0-9626730-5-6

Periodicals
747 General Description. Boeing Commercial Airplane Group, 747 Division, 1972.
747 Structures. Boeing Commercial Airplane Group, Everett Division, undated.
747/747SP Reference Guide. Boeing Commercial Airplane Company, 1976.
747SP Airplane. The Boeing Company, 1980.
747SP Combi. Boeing Commercial Airplane Company, 1977.
747SP General Description. Boeing Commercial Airplane Company, 1975.
747SP Versus DC-10-30. (sales handbook). Boeing Commercial Airplane Company, 1974.
Airliner. Boeing Commercial Airplane Company (various dates).
Annual Report-1975. The Boeing Company, 1976.
Boeing News (various issues).
Boeing 747SP: Certified and in Service. Boeing Commercial Airplane Company, 1976.
Boeing 747SP: Report at Rollout. Boeing Commercial Airplane Company, 1975.
Imperial Iranian Air Force 1. Boeing Commercial Airplane Company, 1977.
New Highways in the Sky. Boeing Commercial Airplane Company, 1976.
U.S. Standard Jet Transport Characteristics. The Boeing Company, 1991.

The following magazines and periodicals were sources of additional information:
ACAR International: Airline & Commercial Aircraft Report; Air Photographic International; Air Transport World; Airliners Magazine; Aviation International News; Aviation-Letter; Aviation Week & Space Technology; Captain's Log (World Airline Historical Society); Flight International; Official Airline Guide, International Edition; World Airline Fleets News

Web Sites
747SP: http://www.algonet.se/~vikingse/SP/
ABN: The Aircraft For Sale Directory; http://www.aircraftworld.com/abn/direct/index.html
NASA/SOFIA: http://sofia.arc.nasa.gov/
National Transportation Safety Board (NTSB): http://www.ntsb.gov